WINTER JOURNEY

Jaume Cabré

WINTER JOURNEY

Translated by Patricia Lunn

SWAN ISLE PRESS
CHICAGO

Jaume Cabré is a novelist, essayist, screenwriter, playwright, and philologist. Among his works are the novels *La teranyina, Fra Junoy o l'agonia dels sons, Senyoria, L'ombra de l'eunuc,* and *Les veus del Pamano.*

Patricia Lunn is professor emerita in the Department of Spanish and Portuguese at Michigan State University. She is coauthor of *En otras palabras,* and *Investigación de gramática,* as well as other works on Spanish and Catalan.

Swan Isle Press, Chicago 60640-8790

©2009 by Swan Isle Press
All rights reserved. Published 2009

Printed in the United States of America
First Edition

13 12 11 10 09   12345
ISBN-13: 978-0-9748881-6-3 (cloth)

Originally published in the Catalan as *Viatge d'Hivern*
©Raval Edicions, S.L.U., PROA, Barcelona, 2001
Peu de la Creu, 4, 08001 Barcelona
www.proa.cat
The Catalan text on which this translation is based has been licensed to Swan Isle Press by Raval Edicions, S..L.U., PROA, Barcelona.

Illustration: Leonard Beard

Library of Congress Cataloging-in-Publication Data

Cabré, Jaume,
  [Viatge d'hivern. English]
  Winter journey / Jaume Cabré ; translated by Patricia Lunn.
    192 p. 15 x 22 cm.
  ISBN 978-0-9748881-6-3 (alk. paper)
  I. Lunn, Patricia V. (Patricia Vining), II. Title.
  PC3942.13.A25V5313 2009
  849'.9354--dc22
                    2009036272

Swan Isle Press gratefully acknowledges that this book has been made possible, in part, with the support of generous grants from:

• Institut Ramon Llull
• Spain's Ministry of Culture and United States Universities and Program for Cultural Cooperation
• The Illinois Arts Council, A State of Illinois Agency
• Europe Bay Giving Trust

www.swanislepress.com

To Margarida

Contents

WINTER JOURNEY

OPUS POSTUM

The Röderleins, because the performer was their professor, held out, though they were in agony, until the twelfth variation. The individual wearing the two vests fled at the fifteenth.

E.T.A. Hoffmann

He adjusted the seat because it was a little low. Though half an hour ago he'd left it just right. No, now it's too high. And it's a little wobbly, see? Damn. Now. No. Yes. He took the handkerchief out of the pocket of his tailcoat and dried the palms of his hands. While he was at it he passed the handkerchief over the spotless keys, as if they were wet from the sweat of other disconcerts. He adjusted his cuffs. Every part of me hurts. My throat is dry, my blood prickles and my heart is about to explode for all kinds of reasons. I don't want my hands to shake. To his right, the mortal chill of the audience. He didn't want to look again in case he really hadn't been disoriented when he sneaked a peek at the first rows while taking a bow. Of course he had. Otherwise, he should stop right now. A woman coughed. A man coughed, far away and hard, which reminded him how huge the hall was. It's nothing, to my right there's nothing going on, nothing. Just ice, the enemy, death. The seat, back, just a little.

High up in the back balcony, hours away from the stage, a woman with honey-and-amber eyes was suffering, hidden by the shadow of the hall, because Pere Bros had been wiping the fear from his hands for four minutes, and the crowd that filled the

3

Auditori and silently watched all of his movements was starting to get nervous.

Pere Bros adjusted his cuffs for the second time. To his right, he felt the absurd and suicidal attraction of nothing, but he resisted it. Then, two fat drops of sweat slid down his forehead and suddenly clouded his vision, and the honey-and-amber eyes in the balcony filled with tears for poor Pere. They don't realize he's suffering, they don't realize this is torture for him. Bros had to take his handkerchief out again and wipe his eyes. Then, with an infinite effort, he covered his face with his hands, conjured up the absurd vision he'd had while taking his bow, and could think only of death. He took a couple of breaths and began with the first mysterious chords of the 960, and a wave of panic passed through the audience. What's he doing, why is he beginning with the last one? The program says... The guy's nuts, why is he doing the program backwards? And the amber eyes listened attentively to the intimate meditation on death, one of life's most thrilling sonatas, with words by Wesselényi that she didn't know, an intimate meditation on death, written by a man who did his crying in B-flat major.

Forty-two minutes and thirteen seconds later, no one in the Auditori was asking why he'd begun at the end. Rather, they were keeping their souls open, waiting, waiting. When the last note had faded away and Pere Bros was holding his hands outstretched above the keyboard, like a demiurge demonstrating his miraculous powers, he achieved ten, fifteen long seconds of silence, for the first and last time in his career. Then he relaxed his posture, lowered his hands, exhausted, and the audience began to applaud. Pere Bros got up, glanced towards the chill on his right, and yes, he saw him again, in the front row, wearing those stylish little spectacles, with his broad forehead and curly hair, dressed inappropriately, in seat number seven, in the silence of the dead and looking right at him, watching from the infinite how people were applauding enthusiastically and no doubt accusing him of not having been up to it. Cold sweat. Pere Bros left the stage to the sounds of public approbation. While he was returning to center stage and bowing his head to acknowledge the applause, it occurred to him that Schubert in the flesh looked just like the portrait on the first page of *Voyage d'hiver*, the detailed and unreliable biography published by Gaston Laforgue at the beginning of the twentieth century. As he made the required exit, he thought of Laforgue's argument that the three 1828 sonatas, the so-called posthumous ones, were written in a frenzy of vanity when Schubert learned that Beethoven had just died and the way was now open before him. His hands sweating, as if he were at the keyboard, he went out again and the applause got louder. I can't play anymore. I want Schubert to go away. They should get him out of the Auditori. I can't play in front of him, for God's sake. And he bowed. Then he thought of that day at the Graben in Vienna, with a cup of very hot chocolate in front of him, when dear Zoltán Wesselényi said, What frenzy, Peter? Schubert left sketches, drafts, doubts, corrections and many questions about the three sonatas: that's no frenzy. (Wesselényi had scalded his tongue because the chocolate was still steaming. My Zoltán, always so dreamy, so sad.) Schubert knew what he was doing, Peter, and he knew he was meditating on his own death. Especially in the D.960.

"Fabulous, my boy. But you're a son of a bitch," spit Pardo as he pushed him onto the stage for another bow.

When he came back the audience was still applauding, but he made a motion to the stage manager to shut the door, he wasn't going back out.

"I don't want to play any more matinees."

"We only have the one on December thirteenth. And it's sold out. What are you complaining about?"

"I'm going to my dressing room," he said, as if this were the complaint.

"You have visitors. Madame Grossman."

"I don't want to see anybody."

"Madame Grossman."

"Nobody."

"And why the hell did you change the order of the program?"

"When the concert is over I want a taxi at the door."

"No way. After the concert you have Madame Grossman and an interview."

"No, I have a taxi."

"Like I said, you're a son of a bitch."

The andante sostenuto of the 960 is death from out of the fog of the Danube, at first far away and then terribly close, and Pere Bros achieved just one moment of tension during the three minutes of exposition, in a very gradual crescendo, impossible to maintain for anyone without hands of gold and fingers tipped with diamonds. And when the theme was repeated, the silence he achieved was so intense that he could hear the wood on the walls of the hall breathing. For that reason, and only for that reason, he did nothing but smile at Pardo and head for his dressing room, followed by his offended agent. He shut the door in his face. Me, without me he has no voice, no memory, no schedule!

Pere Bros poured himself a glass of Veuve Ambal as if this were just one more recital, no problem. But he couldn't keep from weeping. He went over to the upright piano and passed his hands lovingly over the keyboard. He took another sip, sat down at the instrument and raised the lid, utterly dejected. Then he saw the package that had arrived just before he went on stage. Urgent, airmail, from Vienna. He ripped it open. Beautiful, the way the book had turned out. On the cover, the Franciscan church in Vienna where Fischer had played the organ for thirty-three years. And a dedication from Zoltán: "To Pere Bros, who gave me the greatest joy of my life by telling me that he still considered exemplary, twenty-five years later, my version of the D.960. From someone who was not brave enough to pursue the inhuman career of solo performance. May the beloved figure of Schubert and the gigantic figure of Fischer protect us. Your friend, Zoltán Wesselényi."

He took another sip of the champagne and looked back, way back.

Zoltán Wesselényi was playing B-flat, A, D-flat, B, C on the old piano in the archives where he spent all his time since he'd gotten sad. He repeated Fischer's theme and went over to the window.

Outside, a sudden, strange, Mediterranean downpour fell from the Vienna sky.

"What's that?"

"The central theme."

"Didn't you say Fischer died in 1828?"

In response, the musicologist pointed to the papers. They were yellowed by time, but perfectly conserved. The scores were neat, done in a careful hand. It was strange music, lovingly written. Bros was amazed at how how Fischer, starting with that unusual little theme, had constructed a sarabande in G major. Or maybe in ...

"It doesn't have a key. What's it in?"

"I don't know. It's not tonal. Or modal."

"That's impossible."

"No. That's how it is."

"It's beautiful."

"It's brilliant. And I can't stop wondering how he could write like this at the time of Mozart and Beethoven."

The development of the theme was made up of two sections of sixteen measures, each consisting of four phrases of sarabande two measures long, all based on the impossible theme. It was impeccable, masterful.

The two friends were silent for a long time, listening to the out-of-tune sound of the rain. Some drops from the squall were dripping on a metal object that had been left on the floor and making an insistent pinging in C sharp. It was irritating.

"This is really something," Bros said after a half hour of reading the seven variations.

"I'm going to publish it right away. This Fischer, without even trying, walks over Brahms and Wagner, goes beyond Mahler and stands before Schönberg. He wants to transform music before its possibilities are even exhausted."

"But he doesn't release it until he's dying."

"He must have been afraid of how people would react."

"He didn't destroy it, though." Pere Bros looked his friend in the eye. "And what if this is a fake? Have you thought that it might be a fraud?"

"That's the first thing I thought of, and I've had everything analyzed. The paper and the ink are from then, there's no doubt about it."

"Will you let me play it?"

When, after sundown, he took leave of his friend, he confessed that he was still moved by the memory of the D.960 he'd played at the Konservatorium, and he added in a lower voice and into his ear, My dear Zoltán, why did you give up performing when you're the best? Hmm? Why, when you're my compass?

He hugged him hard, as if he wanted his embrace to explain many other things. Wesselényi broke free, smiled and said, Look, things happen. And to change the subject he promised that when the book on Fischer came out, he'd send it to him by special delivery wherever he was. If in return he'd read it and comment on it.

Pere Bros poured himself another glass of Veuve Ambal. Someone was knocking impatiently at the dressing room door. He paid no attention. He played B-flat, A, D-flat, B, C over and over on the upright. Three years had gone by since that find in the Vienna Archives, but he knew the theme and the development by heart. Then the door burst open. Pardo, red in the face and making heroic efforts not to explode, closed it behind him.

"What's the game? Madame Grossman says that... asks me to tell you she'd give anything to be able to play like you." Energetically, "She's excited and we have to take advantage of it."

"Tell her I've given my life to be able to play like me."

"No, no, no. No." Being reasonable was giving him a headache. "I'm trying to get her to double our fee for anything in France. Watch what you're doing and be nice to her."

"Get her out of here. Oh, and I'm not going out for the second part."

Pardo looked at how much was left in the bottle, took the glass out of his hands and said in a neutral voice:

"You said that ten times already. Okay, you've messed with me enough. Everybody has stage fright sometimes.

"But we all have a limit. And today I reached mine."

"You played beautifully."

"I died beautifully." He wanted to say that he was sad. He wanted to shout it. But not at Pardo. He wanted to go to Vienna and say, It's over, Zoltán, no more traveling, no more thinking about what might have been; I've finally chosen between music and you. And you've won, in spite of your indifference, in spite of all the hours of work and practice that I'm thowing away, in spite of the sweet praise and applause and honors. That's what he wanted to say, more or less. And he wanted him to say, Oh, good, Peter.

"Why did you play the last sonata first?" burst out Pardo.

"I don't know. It just occurred to me. As if it were an ending. I was very..." His voice changed a little. "Schubert was in the first row. Seat seven."

When he heard this, Pardo gave him back the glass.

"It's better for you to drink. But not too much. Remember that Madame Grossman is outside with a friend of hers. This is important: double the fee. We can put off the reporter until tomorrow."

"I said I'm quitting."

"Having a full schedule this spring depends on little things like, for example, not seeing ghosts, not walking out of recitals in the middle, smiling at Madame Grossman and listening politely to her compliments."

"You can tell her to stuff them up her ass."

"If you don't go out for the second part, I know I'll have a heart attack."

They looked at one another for twenty seconds, long enough for both of them to remember the years of poverty, of endless traveling, of arguments, of earnings, of the days of happiness and tears that bound them together. Pardo pointed to the door and said in an encouraging voice, Shall I ask her to come in?

Pere Bros turned away contemptuously and Pardo, pale with rage, left the dressing room, closed the door, smiled broadly at the two impatient women and described, in Dantean terms, the sudden stomach problems suffered by poor Bros—who, meanwhile, was pouring himself more champagne in the dressing room. His hand was shaking. It had been shaking for thirty-eight years, since when he was nine and beginning with Srta. Trullols, until he was forty-seven and raising a full glass of Veuve Ambal. He drank to his health, to all the hours of practicing to be always perfect, inhuman, warm, human, brilliant, forceful, convincing, intense, subtle, tender, impeccable; always, always, always, always. So many hours with his nose to the grindstone, for nothing, now that he was saying Enough in a little room with a mirror surrounded by a thousand light bulbs, in the middle of a recital. So many hours of practicing and being afraid of Schubert. Get him out of here, he said softly to the encouraging glass. Kick him out. It's not right!

The intermission was ending, and Pardo came into the dressing room silently, sat down and waited for some kind of violent reaction. But Bros didn't even look at him; he just sat and drank. So Pardo decided to go on the attack.

"So all of a sudden you can't deal with stage fright?"

"You don't have to live with it; I do." Raising his voice, "Did you see Schubert?"

"There's no Schubert in the hall! I went and looked, I swear."

"He probably went out to the lobby to smoke a cigar. I can't go out if he's listening to me."

"You can't just turn your back on music!"

"I'm not turning my back on music. Just on performing."

"Listen, we can talk tomorrow about quitting, and we'll do whatever you say... But today... You have to finish the recital. And then, Madame Grossman."

"No."

"And you're going to quit like this, in the middle of a concert?"

"Yes. I don't even enjoy practicing because I'm thinking about how awful the concert's going to be. I can't stand so much stress. I've never been able to deal with so much stress."

"You've always gotten through things. Always!" Begging, "Isn't that guarantee enough?"

"I make music to be happy. Playing in public stopped making me happy a long time ago. And today..."

"Who says music is supposed to make you happy?" Pardo interrupted him, enraged. "It doesn't make me happy either, and I put up with it."

Bros looked at his face: Pardo wasn't being funny. He watched his agent, who hated champagne, pour himself a glass and he understood why he was doing it.

"Don't worry, I'm not trying to get drunk. I'm making this decision with a clear head."

Pardo realized that this crisis was different from the others and decided not to use the curses and insults he had on hand. He pretended to take a sip of champagne and put down the glass. Since Bros was just looking at him in silence, he began to enumerate: First, you don't know how to do anything else than perform.

"I can rest. I can give lessons."

"Second, you don't have any fucking idea how to give lessons. You've never earned your living by giving lessons; you've never had enough patience to give lessons."

While Pardo was going on to number three, Bros thought that that wasn't true, for a few weeks he'd given lessons to his neighbor, a very sweet girl, very... I don't know, very.

"Are you sure it doesn't bother you when I practice?"

"No! We like it. When you... , my mother and I... we even stop talking, so we can hear better. And we love to talk." In a lower voice, "What I don't like is when you're away."

"But then it's quiet. This time I'm going to be gone for a couple of weeks."

"Don't go."

"What?"

"No, I..."

The girl looked right at him, with her bright amber eyes, beautiful, and wondered why he wasn't even aware she existed, a man so... so...

"Don't worry. When I get back we'll do some extra classes."

"No, that's not what I meant. It's..."

"You have talent. But you should look for a better teacher. Somebody organized, who knows how to give lessons. I'm very..."

"I want to be... study with you. Only you. Always."

His only student. One day when he was feeling very weak and very alone he told her how he suffered before every concert. And she, with those eyes, understood him in silence and didn't dare to take his hand. They were strange, those lessons, irregular but intense sessions that went on for almost three years. They ended when he changed apartments and stopped thinking about the girl and the lessons. Until today. What was her name?

Then the bell rang and Pardo stood up, very tense, having gotten to number five, which had to do with professional responsibility and our long friendship and you can't do this without jeopardizing the whole thing and if you'd gotten married you'd be a lot more stable. He gave up on the speech and said in a neutral tone:

"The first bell. You should..."

Pere Bros made a gesture that could have meant anything. Pardo decided that maybe it meant Fine, I give up, I agree. So Bros wouldn't feel pressured, he left him alone in the dressing room.

Pere Bros knew the number of the Musikwissenschaftzentrum by heart from the many, many times he'd opened his address book, spent a few minutes thinking, I don't have any right to interfere, but now that he's lost Anna, I... , and the many times he'd dialled the number and hung up before the secretary answered and said, What can I do for you, Herr Bros.

"I want to talk with Herr Wesselényi. It's urgent."

He wasn't there and she was very sorry. But because it was urgent, she gave him the number of his cell phone and Pere found him somewhere in Vienna, sounding a little distracted: Hey; Peter, what do you want, and he said, No, nothing, just thanks for the book about Fischer. I've only been able to flip through it, but you can tell it's amazing. And he stopped talking to let Wesselenyi express some interest. But he did nothing more than ask the conventional question.

"I can't play," Pere Bros confessed, finally. "And I can't not play." After an uncomfortable silence, "I think about you a lot. I'm sad, Zoltán."

It made him feel very bad that Wessenlényi kept his distance and he thought, Why are you always so cold, Zoltán. To get a reaction from him, he said, "I haven't slept in six months because I'm so upset and I need some rest. And you told me..."

Zoltán's answer disarmed him: he asked if they could talk some other time, which made Pere desperate because his friend didn't realize it was now or never. He tried to make him react. "You told me, if music keeps you from being happy, quit music."

"Listen, we'll talk about this, all right?"

Pere searched desperately for a gambit that would keep the conversation going. He found it. "I've seen Schubert."

"Schubert?"

The hesitation that Pere noticed was too long. So long that he felt humiliated and had to say something.

"Fine, fine," he said in a cutting tone, perhaps of surrender.

"Call me some other time, all right?"

"I love you, Zoltán. With all my heart. Remember that."

He hung up so as not to feel the disappointment of the cold response, and thought, Life is a bitch. The man I love is always a thousand miles from my hotel and my desire and he doesn't even know how I long for him. He finished the glass of champagne and waited for the second bell, seemingly resigned.

When the second bell rang, Pardo was saying good-bye to Madame Grossman. When he was free, he went back to the dressing room prepared to drag Bros out if he had to. The room was empty, as if Bros had decided to run away. Pardo felt scared and was seized by a premonition as strong as a battery of heart attacks, which made him even more scared, and he left the dressing room ready to hunt down the pianist and kill him or else to fall on his knees in front of somebody and say he was sorry about whatever they said he should be sorry about. When the third bell rang, he heard applause in the hall. That was odd. He went to the door and opened it a little, to the disapproval of the stage manager, and looked out. People were still rushing in, wondering what the hurry was. Pere Bros was already there, bowing with his eyes shut. Pardo, calmer now, thought that maybe he needed a vacation. And with things moving and one more crisis behind him, he went into a corner with his cell phone because he had to finalize the date for Bros, that nut, to play a recital at the Vatican.

What's going on? thought Amber Eyes. B-flat, A, D-flat, B, C. That's not Schubert. Two seconds later, when the sarabande began, there was a rustle in the hall, accompanied by I told you he was crazy, completely nuts; and an offended If I'd known this was going to be modern I wouldn't have come, this is a trick; and Do you recognize this, because in the program it says... Hey, I'm here to listen to the three Schubert sonatas from 1828! In the back balcony, Amber Eyes was afraid because the angry man who was saying that Bros was crazy was probably right. Crazy from so much pressure, that only she knew about, her sweet secret, if only she could help him. Whistling broke out on one side of the front balcony, but the polite contingent of the audience managed to silence the protest. Bros was on the second variation, with Wessenlényi's book open like a score. Then Pardo, who was on the phone ruling out dates and times with Monsignor Walzer, a shadowy and obscure Vatican bishop, became aware of the music he'd been listening to for some time, and his heart lurched because what that son of a bitch Bros was playing wasn't Schubert by any stretch of the imagination. His swearing scandalized his Vatican interlocutor, who was simply trying to make sure he had a pianist for a private recital in the Santa Clara salon. Yes, you can count on that, Monsignor.

The first variation: he'd never heard anything like it, ever. It's not a harmonic development of the theme; it's certainly not a main melody that modulates towards distant tonalities. It's... *Mein Gott*, I would never have thought anyone could make music like this. The harmonic patterns of the melodic theme and the melodic patterns of the harmony are woven together. How strange. There's no tonic, no relationship between major and minor, just music floating in the air. *Mein Gott*. What ugly and strange perfection. But... and my sonatas? Why doesn't he play the first sonata from 1828?

Second variation: the knowlegeable members of the audience were exchanging even more worried glances, and a deep, clear voice from the thirteenth row could be heard saying, I don't know what this guy's playing, but it's bullshit.

Third variation: three people get up. Rows four and eight. They stand there for a few seconds to express their disapproval of this lack of respect for Schubert. This bold move prompts seven or eight other people to stand up, in various places in the hall. For a few seconds it looks as if the representatives of a majestic parliament are voting in the traditional way. But Pere Bros wasn't counting the votes because he was deeply involved with the fourth variation, a movement that imitated four voices, almost a minuet. And many of the representatives called for silence and asked the other members of the chamber to refrain from rowdiness and listen, because it was beautiful. It wasn't Schubert, true, but it was beautiful.

By the fifth variation, the board of the Auditori was meeting in room 2A of the lobby with Bros's agent to talk about what the hell you can do when these things happen. Thus they came to the seventh variation, fairly short, very pianistic, a recapitulation, very showy and, yes, it was something you just had to listen to.

"Does anybody know what this is?"

"No idea. But it's very nice."

"I once heard something like this by Berio."

"No, come on. Ligeti. It's Ligeti, but I don't know what."

"Pardo, isn't there anything you can do about this?"

"What do you want me to do? Go out on stage and drag him off?"

"You think it's Ligeti?"

"Yeah, or somebody like that."

"I'm going to sue him. For breach of contract."

"Are you okay, Pardo? Here, hold him up... Call a doctor, right away."

"Christ, what a day."

Ligeti or somebody like that, or whoever it was, went right from the last variation to a repetition of the theme, almost like a shy and delicate joke, and the story ended as it had begun. And at the end, the five notes of the theme, naked, sad, and silence.

Pere Bros got up, pale from audacity and exertion. But it was a thousand times easier to play something that wasn't Schubert in front of Schubert. Now he could look right at him. All of a sudden he realized that Schubert, in seat seven, was on his feet and applauding enthusiastically. The audience, though, was silent. Franz Schubert smiled while continuing to applaud and Bros noticed that he had a tooth missing. Still no sound from the audience. All of a sudden, from the back balcony, far away, there was amber clapping, energetic and sweet at the same time, as if that person, whoever it was, wanted to express sympathy with the invisible and silent Schubert, or with Fischer's daring, or perhaps with the mad painist. Little by little more applause broke out until, like a shower that turns into a downpour, the entire audince was on its feet. Pere Bros held up the book, with the name Fischer in big letters, made sure that Schubert was still applauding, and left the stage for the last time without looking back.

THE WILL

The blows of the mallet against the stone sounded extremely cruel. They hadn't had a headstone ready because nobody is ready for death. Especially not a healthy person like her. He was the one who was sick and had spent the last few months going from one doctor to another. He was the one who thought death was just around the corner, not Eulalia. Who for the last week had stumbled from one test to another with his head full of scary thoughts. How could he understand Eulalia's death, except as one of fate's unfortunate mistakes?

The undertakers finished their work and Agustí felt desperately alone among his children and his friends, without Eulalia who has filled my life, my hours, my desires, always with her welcoming smile, always willing to understand me, always by my side, my love, giving much and receiving little, my love. He was distracted by Amadeu moving away from the group and, attentive as usual, discreetly putting a folded bill into the hand of the man in charge, who murmured his thanks.

Agustí would have liked to say some closing words. He would have liked to explain to everyone present that Eulalia had been the light of his life, and that these words were an inadequate testimony to his desperate love. But no sooner did he open his mouth than his soul was filled with tears. Amadeu put his hand on his back, gently, perhaps to make him feel that he was not alone in his sorrow. Then he realized that all three of his children were around him, looking dazedly at the rough stone that would always hide the memory of the mother who had died suddenly at the age of fifty. All of them together. Agustí couldn't help thinking about the twenty-nine years of peaceful marriage, about the children who didn't come until, almost without warning, one arrived and was Amadeu... And after a long interlude, Carla was born. Not long after that they had their first real conflict, when he'd gotten carried away with a younger woman, very different from Eulalia; but things had settled down and, almost as a result, after Carla had turned five, Sergi came, his favorite. He looked at him now: at fifteen, he was the one with the fewest defenses against the death of his mother. He was letting his sister put her arm around him. Carla had always been a mystery to her father; she'd left home when she turned eighteen and lived for two years in Florence and in Munich, documented and connected by a total of six postcards, and now she'd been back for a few months, as if she'd returned for the express purpose of being on time for her mother's funeral. She said she'd come back to study art at the Autònoma, but he was convinced that the real reason was a problem with some man. She wasn't coming back but running away. She'd grown beautiful in these two years. Carla had always been pretty; it was hard to believe she was his daughter. And Amadeu, now paying more attention to his wife's belly than to the tail end of the burial. With an efficiency that he'd always secretly envied, Amadeu had made sure that everything stayed on track to spare his father the hateful finality of bereavement, and, almost without realizing it, Agustí found himself on the way to the car, the gravel crunching beneath his feet, feeling strangely guilty for leaving Eulalia alone, abandoned, forgotten. Because now was the hard part: living without her, making Sergi believe that the two of them would get along fine without Mother.

"Come and eat with us," his daughter-in-law offered.

"No." And in justification, "We have to start getting used to it. Right, Sergi?"

"Bye, Dad." Carla and her quick kiss.

He was about to try and trick her into staying by telling her that he was sick, that in the afternoon he was going to find out the results of half of the tests, that he was really scared, that he wanted her with him now that Eulalia was gone, that...

"If you need anything, honey..."

"Me? No..." In her best style, "I'll call you, okay?" And, more energetically, messing her brother's hair with her hand, "Bye, Sergi."

At least he hadn't tried to trick her. But in the afternoon he had to go to the doctor, with Carla or without her; there was no getting around it.

He'd left home too early, impatient to hear the verdict, and he found himself outside the hospital an hour before his appointment with the doctor. He felt like an idiot for being obsessed with his own expiration date. With an hour to kill before the death sentence, he headed for the Cafe Vienna, thinking about Eulalia and how he'd like to have her come with him and distract him by talking about anything that wasn't health-related... How unfair. How terribly unfair to say that he needed her without thinking that she was the one living in the frozen realm. Then he walked by the Fundació, read the banners about the exposition, and didn't think any more about the café or, for a few moments, even about sorrow.

The entire room was dominated by dark ochres, and his eyes went automatically to the window on the right that, more than a place to look out of, was an entryway for the strong, bold sunlight that lit up the chamber and the man. He was a philosopher, as the title of the painting explained, seated at a round table covered with a cloth and reading a huge book full of wisdom, by the heaven-sent light that had been coming from the window since Rembrandt painted him four centuries ago. The philosopher's beard came halfway down his chest and his whole being radiated a feeling of calm, of peacefulness, of I'm not sick and I don't have to go to the doctor to get a death notice, and nobody I know has died. Across from the window, in the same room, he could make out stairs that went down from that ivory tower to the world of hurry and sickness and the unexpected death of poor, dear Eulalia. In the foreground, more felt than seen, a huge bookcase full of volumes as big as the one on the table. Why couldn't I be that philosopher?

He looked at the twenty-six paintings that the Nasjonalgalleriet of Oslo was exhibiting in various European cities to advertise itself and stimulate tourism in Norway. For a few happy minutes he forgot about his fear of the sentence, Eulalia's fateful demise, Carla's coldness, Sergi's rebellious tears, Amadeu's silence... and thought that living surrounded by such beauty was a gift. And without thinking about it he went back to the painting of the philosopher five or six times, as if he wanted to discover, by looking at it intently, the fount of true wisdom. He was so involved that he forgot about the time, and when he finally looked at his watch, he was already late for his appointment at the hospital. He left the Fundació in a rush, almost running into a policeman who, with some pleasure, was giving tickets to a string of cars that must have been illegally parked, and reached the hospital panting, scared, afraid that he'd be punished for being seventeen minutes late by having to remain in doubt for twenty-four more hours, and, still panting, asked for the doctor at the reception desk. Which doctor? The one who's supposed to tell me the hour and the day of my death. Fourth floor.

He only had to wait for ten long minutes, along with twenty other condemned prisoners who were probably as scared as he was. The time he'd spent in contemplation at the Fundació had strengthened his will, and he promised himself that, no matter what the results of the tests, at night he'd watch a little TV with Sergi and in two or three days take him to the movies. Out of love for the child, out of love for Eulalia. He'd have time to cry by himself later, now that he was getting used to the cruel claws of loneliness.

"Please sit down."

He sat down across from the doctor, who made no mention of his tardiness. Like an idiot, he stared at the pencils in the pocket of her very white coat, as if that's where all the answers were. The nurse, a hairy young man with permanently shiny eyes, deposited on the table some envelopes which Agustí assumed contained his fate. The slap of the envelopes on the table reminded him of the blows of the mallet on Eulàlia's tombstone. To make things even harder, the young man whispered something to the doctor, who nodded a couple of times, waited for the nurse to disappear through a door that Agustí hadn't noticed, and let two, three, four seconds go by before taking off her glasses and fixing on him a bluish gaze, full of pity. Agustí figured the whole thing meant six months, at the most. With pain.

"All of this is rather strange, Mr. ..."

"Ardèvol." He said it rapidly, in the hope that now she'd look at the envelope, realize her mistake, and see him off with a kiss. "Agustí Ardèvol," he insisted. But no: the doctor picked up the envelope that clearly said Agustí Ardèvol, took out some papers and reread them, and he could see that the woman had already read them thirty times. And he thought about Sergi, abandoned, with no father or mother... And Carla, though it hurt him to know that she wouldn't be very upset by his death... And Amadeu, who could be counted on to take care of everything with his quiet efficiency... How he loved them, his children! Maybe he hadn't said that often enough. Maybe he'd been too reserved, but he loved them with all his heart. He saw the doctor hesitating and, to keep from exploding, he cried impatiently, "Go ahead and tell me, doctor! How many years?" And because she still said nothing, he bravely reduced the time. "How many months do I have?"

"Excuse me?"

"No, I..." Now Agustí felt a little confused. "What do I have?"

"Um... Nothing very bad, Mr. Ardèvol," she said, taking off her glasses. "You're basically healthy."

Agustí fell against the back of the chair, horrified. Either she was teasing him, or he had not years or months or days, but only a few hours left, and so she wanted to keep him from knowing right up to the end... Dear Eulalia... if there's anything after, which there isn't, I'll see you soon. The memory of your love is surely what is making it possible to keep from panicking. Amadeu, Carla, Sergi, your father will try to die in a dignified way, he'll try to deserve to be remembered as a worthy husband to your mother. I love you.

Then he heard the doctor's voice, which was explaining the results of the various tests in comprehensible language; no problem here, no problem there. She read him the riot act about trans fat and the dangers of bad cholesterol, about the need to live frugally, eat a lot of vegetables, cut down on drinking and smoking. He interrupted her with the question inside him.

"So I'm not dying?"

Instead of answering, the doctor responded with another question, as if they were playing tennis.

"You're married, with children, right?"

"Well..." It was the first time he'd had to talk about it and he had to take a deep breath first. "My wife died the day before yesterday. Cerebral hemorrhage." And, as an excuse, "We buried her today."

"My goodness." She took off her glasses. "You have my sympathy."

"Thank you."

"You have three children, right?"

How many times had the doctor taken off her glasses? As he was saying Yes, three children, he couldn't remember her having put them on, as if she were wearing thirty or forty pairs for those moments when she had to say something important. Like now, when she took them off and turned her blue eyes towards Agustí's suspicious face.

"The thing is that... It's quite surprising, but the results..." She waved one of the papers. "...don't leave any room for doubt."

"Come on, doctor..." Now he tried to recover a little of his self-esteem with an attempt at humor. "Look, the truth is that now I know I'm not going to die... nothing you say can hurt me or scare me."

She looked at him as if she had doubts about her patient's mental balance. She sighed, looked at the clock behind Agustí's head, and decided to get down to it.

"Well, as I was saying," and she shoved the paper across the table so it landed in front of him, took off her glasses—yes, again—and looked at him as she said, "I can tell you for sure that since you had that high fever... since you had the mumps..." Now she picked up the paper and finally Agustí realized that she was putting on her glasses and reading, "...when you were, uh, fifteen, you've been sterile."

Uncomfortable, the doctor took off her glasses and put them down on the table. The sound they made reminded him of the blows on Eulalia's stone. Agustí, his mouth open, thought... He couldn't think anything because he was beginning to accept that the fate of survivors can also be extremely cruel.

WITH HOPE IN HIS HANDS

Don't tell me it's not true that the sun bathes in the sea.
Feliu Formosa

"Because I want to see the sunset again from the Sau Valley."
"That seems like a stupid kind of reason for risking your life."

"When I was young, I came back from Saxony because I was homesick."

"You'll always be a fool."

"Yes. I'll always miss Sau."

The two men were standing under the savage sun, which fell hard on the back of their necks, taking their time to empty the stinking content of their pails, making it look like the shit was sticking, delaying a little longer and keeping their voices low, so no one would imagine they were having a conversation under that cruel sun. Oleguer truly did miss Sau and its imposing landscape. But what really consumed him, and the reason for the whole thing, was finding out why Celia didn't write to him. Twelve years of rats and cockroaches, waiting every day, every minute, every second of his life for a letter that never came.

"You've never seen a sunset in Sau," he replied to Tonet, so as not to have to bring Celia into the conversation.

"I don't need to. I don't want to escape. If they find out, they'll kill you before they ask a single question. I don't want to know anything about it. You haven't told me anything." And he turned to leave with his empty but still stinking pail. Oleguer raised his head, discouraged, and saw that mean-faced soldier looking right at him, a sprig of rosemary in his mouth, his eyes bright with hatred of all the pitiful bastards locked up in the prison of the glorious King Ferran.

Six years ago, when planning the first attempt to get out, he hadn't kept anything back and had told his secret to Massip, the one he'd chosen for the escape, who, chewing on a blade of dry grass, had replied, Very nice, but what you should do is forget all about your damn daughter.

"Don't call her damned. 1 don't know why she doesn't write to me."

"Because she doesn't care a fig about you."

"No: she might be busy. She might've gotten married, maybe she has lots of children and..."

"You're an idiot," Massip had answered. "But 1 wish 1 had a daughter to miss. And who knew how to write, on top of it. And forget about escaping. I'm afraid to try."

At the time, Oleguer Gaulter had been forced to give up on the idea, because he couldn't carry out his plan alone and he knew that the only person with whom he could do it was Massip, the only prisoner for whom he would put his hand in the fire. The rest of them, if they knew about it in advance, would give away the plot to gain some tiny advantage with the warden. For if those walls had succeeded in anything, it was in degrading everyone inside to the point of taking away their sense of shame.

How things change: seven months later, Massip begged him to explain the escape plan, because of an emergency. They could talk in the yard then, in the morning, because the warden at the time had granted them a longer break, despite the unspoken indignation of the sullen jailers and the soldiers in the garrison.

"You'll have to climb out in the dark. It's the same plan."

"1 don't care. That's great."

For three nights, behind the backs of their cellmates, they made sure that more or less at midnight, at the changing of the guard, everyone in the prison was asleep and they could help one another climb onto the roof, using the rope he'd braided with infinite patience out of hope and straw. From there, if they weren't afraid of the fall, the height of two tall men, they could get away across the fields, even if one of them broke a leg, and try to endure the pain until they got to the forest where, unless they were hunted with dogs, they could consider themselves almost safe. Massip, who seven months before had turned up his nose because the plan left too much to chance, had to admit that it was the only way possible. Three days earlier, they'd taken him to the warden's office and read him the official decree. Then he'd gotten the trots and gone running to Oleguer to ask, Hey, friend, what about that plan of yours?

"You'll have to climb out in the dark. It's the same plan."

"I don't care. That's great," Massip had said. "I'll escape with you. And let's do it right away," he added. Oleguer decided it would be the first time when the midnight moon didn't turn the night yellow. Five days, Massip. But everything came to an end because, incomprehensibly, they put the date of the execution forward, and Oleguer's plan and Massip's life were both destroyed. The wretch had taken Oleguer's secret with him to the miserable tomb of the prisoners of the mad king Ferran, the sixth of that name, of the Bourbon line.

And so, and in memory of poor Massip, he'd spoken of the sunset in Sau only to Tonet. Tonet, the shit bucket in his hand, had looked at him askance and moved away. Oleguer, thinking about all of this, stopped leaning against the wall of the yard and went towards the setting sun, where there were no other prisoners to call him crazy. He trusted no one, but if in the end he'd chosen Tonet, it would be Tonet, who was as small and as slight as Massip. He spent the time that hung heavy on his hands thinking of Celia, of those who'd died, of Master Nicolau, of the landscape of Austria and of Saxony, as different as their language, which he'd come to master after the six or seven years he spent there. And when he tired of reviewing his memories, he spent his time perfecting the escape plan he'd explained to Massip. He knew that after midnight, when the watch changed, most of the sentries took the opportunity to get some sleep, because nothing ever happened in the prison and it was so dark that it was impossible to take a step without falling into one of the holes or poorly covered drains in the yard. What the jailers didn't know was that, after twelve years, Oleguer's eyes, besides getting paler—more from hopelessness than from the darkness—had adjusted to seeing in the dark, like cats' eyes. Another thing they didn't know was that, instead of the predictable route through the yard, he planned to go over the roof, where it was impossible to take a step at night without risking your neck. And why doesn't she write to me one single time? Just once?... He'd sent her seven letters during the first seven months. A comment from the previous warden to the effect that she didn't seem to want to answer made him stop writing for a time. For fear of seeming pathetic? No: so as not to annoy her. But a few months later he went back to writing brief, imploring notes, in which he said, Celia, my daughter, just let me know you're alive, that you're well, that you've married, that you have children, that you remember me. Just a sheet of paper saying, Hello, Father. I don't ask for anything else. Hello, Father; it's what I most want in the world, Celia.

Then they changed the warden and put in that bastard Ròdenes, who called himself baron without being one and who enjoyed watching the bodies of his herd grow thin because of the villainy for which they'd been imprisoned. No more walking in the yard and a return to the convent rule of perpetual silence, too much squawking. Then they even forbade writing, or do you think we should burden the royal mail with your drivel? You shouldn't have committed a crime in the first place. And six years went by like that, or maybe seven, waiting every day for Celia's letter. For that reason, and not because he missed the sunsets in Sau, which he could hardly remember, he'd decided to escape from His Majesty's prison.

When he was seven years old, his father, who had moved from Sau to Barcelona, apprenticed him to the workshop of Nicolau Saltor, the master organ builder. Had his father known that, by putting him in contact with Master Saltor, he was condemning his son to a life sentence at the age of forty and to dying, rotten inside and out, locked up in the most squalid penitentiary in the country, he would surely have taken him back. But that's the thing about destiny: it reveals not the whole story, but only the little piece it chooses, and then it misleads you with an ambiguous snicker.

And so, unaware of his fate, Oleguer soon stood out in the workshop of Master Saltor. He was an apprentice for only a short time. At the age of fifteen he was the master's ear in the lengthy process of tuning the pipes, and his hands carressed the metal, the wood and the felt, and his mind penetrated the secrets of the complex mechanical miracle of the sound of the organ and the many ways of configuring an efficient wind-chest. He started to live life through the thousand sounds of the organ and, without realizing it, he was more or less happy.

He was shocked when, the next day, as they were going back after emptying the buckets, Tonet said, Fine, yes, I'm interested. I'm tired of shitting in a pail. But first you have to tell me exactly how it's going to work.

They had to wait until they were in the yard. Sitting in a sunny corner, so no one would bother them, he explained, without wiping at the sweat that ran down him, that he'd had the key to the cell for twelve years, since the day after being locked up. That it had been a piece of luck; a jailer you don't know dropped it in the corridor and nobody realized that it bounced off something and ended up by his feet, inside the cell. He hid it in the straw, without knowing if he'd be able to use it, and after looking for it unsuccessfully, all they did was make a copy of the key instead of changing the lock. And a few months later, by dint of patiently watching the movements of the jailers, he found out that the same key opened the door at the end of the corridor, the one that led to the attic and, through a hole in the chimney, to the roof. For a dozen years, the key had burned in his mind, but he'd been able to keep the secret until it was the right time for the escape. Yes, over the roof. Where they least expected it.

"I won't be able to get through the hole in the chimney."

"Stop eating for a few days. I can get through it."

"If we get onto the roof... we could break our necks."

"Yes. But they don't guard the roof."

The soldier with the gray beard and the sprig of rosemary was observing them from afar, with such a nasty look on his face that it seemed as if he could hear their words. When Tonet had heard everything, he sucked in air, put a hand on Oleguer's back and said, in a whisper, "It's impossible." And after pausing and looking at the soldier who was watching them, "But I'm coming with you. On one condition."

"What."

"That Faner comes with us."

He should have thought of that. Tonet and Faner were always together. They were hand-in-glove, and when he told Tonet about the escape, he hadn't thought of that. He thought through all the steps, imagining them now with Tonet and Faner, who was even scrawnier than Tonet.

"All right, Tonet," he sighed after a moment, "Faner can come if he's willing to break a leg." He smiled wearily and added, "But if he squeals, I'll kill him."

And that was how they decided to escape in two weeks, when the moon was again on the wane. Oleguer spent what were to be his last days in prison sitting, his back against the wall of the cell, his hands clasped behind his neck, thinking of Vienna, which he knew almost better than Barcelona. When King Carles gave up the throne, he called together part of the court he'd had in Barcelona and a group of generals and officers sympathetic to Austria. It was the express wish of the queen that Master Nicolas Saltor go to Vienna as well. Oleguer, only nineteen years old, his parents dead and his eyes eager to see new things, went gladly into voluntary exile as assistant to Master Nicolas, to serve the king who in Vienna became an emperor and changed his name from Carles to Karl and his number from third to sixth.

Then, exactly then, when Oleguer was counting down the days in prison, leaning against the wall with his hands behind his neck, thinking about Vienna, about Celia, about Sau, about the death of Maria, about the terrible news that his heart had told him about Pere, they replaced the bastard Ròdenes. No one breathed for a few days, praying that the routine of the prison wouldn't change, that everything would stay hopelessly the same, and escape would still be possible. And after the forest, if his legs were whole, he'd get a carter to take him to Vic, and the first thing he'd do would be to go to the house to see if Celia still lived there. Or if there were new tenants who could tell him where she'd gone. And he'd look her in the eye and say, Don't worry, I'll leave right away, my dear daughter. I don't want to bother you... But why haven't you written to me even once in twelve years, not even once? Your letters would have given me hope. Just having the paper in my hands, life would have been less painful. The day the troopers came looking for me with an arrest warrant because the framework of the Augustine's organ had collapsed and crushed two friars, I saw your eyes shine like pearls, my darling, with the tears you didn't shed to keep from making things worse. And I only had time to say, Go to Bertrana's house, they'll take you in, it's only for a few days. But it turned out that one of the dead friars was the head of the order, and was some kind of cousin to a minister of the mad king, and the few days had turned into a few years with a recommendation of special treatment. And I kept writing, Sweetheart, how are things at Bertrana's, what are you doing, I'll be back soon. And from you, nothing, And because I hadn't felt my heart skip a beat, I kept on writing.

Because one day, Massip had said, God forbid, but maybe she's dead. And he managed to smile and say, Come on, I would've known, the way I knew about my Maria, who died when he was away from home, repairing the water damage to his organ in the cathedral of Manresa, which took him two months. And while he was tuning, still unsatisfied, the bassoon pedals on the epistle side, he felt his heart skip a beat at the very moment, they told him later, that Maria had given up the ghost all of a sudden, without warning. And when Pere went under the wheels of that cart, he, who was walking from Prats to Moià, with a good contract for the repair of three harmoniums, turned right around, lost the contract and, just as he feared, he'd lost his son and heir. And my heart hasn't skipped a beat, Massip. My Celia is alive and well, but I can't imagine why she doesn't write to me.

They fired Ròdenes and replaced him with a thin, sober and quiet man who kept his candle lit until well after midnight. For the first few days the guards were always exchanging looks, trying to figure out how far they could go and how much trouble the new warden was going to be.

On his cot in the murk, Oleguer was thinking about Celia, and to get her out of his head he reminisced about Vienna, the two years he lived in the still-unfinished Schönbrunn, working on the great organ in the Imperial Chapel, the next-to-last organ signed by Master Saltor before he succumbed to the fever that destroyed him. The emperor had been so pleased with the work he'd done that he gave Master Saltor permission to go and visit all of the organs in the empire and in Germany. A long year spent traveling, listening, playing, remembering, comparing and learning the deepest secrets in the impossible pursuit of the perfect instrument. It was in the year 17, when Oleguer had turned twenty-two, that Master Nicolau Saltor accepted the commission in Markkleeberg and set up a temporary workshop on the green banks of the Pleisse. With unusual rapidity he built a positive organ that was not very large but produced an angelic sound, for the town's Lutheran church. Oleguer knew that it was the best organ his master had ever made. And the master was glad to leave a sample of his talent in an unknown and lovely Saxon town. He had a metal plaque engraved with *Saltorius barcinonensis me fecit, anno 1718*, and he died, happy.

A week later, Oleguer felt sure that the escape plan was still workable. He informed the other two conspirators, who, on the sly and with great difficulty, were making a thin rope from wisps of straw from their pallets. And they agreed that there would be a new moon on Friday the seventeenth and they would escape that night, even if there was a thunderstorm. What they hadn't taken into account was the new warden's capacity for work.

The day came; the night came. With beating hearts, they waited for the other occupants of the cell to go to sleep and the jailer's light to grow dim as he went down the passage, so they could breathe freely and take the key from its hiding place. Their cellmates, one after another, began to snore peacefully; but that night the jailer's light, instead of growing dim as it was supposed to do, as it had done for thousands of nights, grew stronger. And, horrified, they saw that someone was opening their door. The jailer, the one whose mouth was black with cavities, pointed at him and said, You. And he smiled a cruel smile, showing his devastated teeth. The other two were breathless with fear; Oleguer was crushed. He didn't know how they could have found out about the escape plan. He looked at his co-conspirators accusingly, but they were too terrified to raise their eyes. Resigned, he followed the jailer and thought, I'll never see Celia's pearly eyes again. If only she'd sent me one letter... Like lightning the image of Master Saltor's burial flashed in his mind, and his decision to take on the commissions that his master had accepted in Markkleeberg, and the sensation of being all alone in the world because his parents were gone and his master too, and he was alone to say yes or no, to go right or left, to bang his head against the wall until it cracked or to go down the long hall that led to the warden's rooms.

The new warden received him in his office, standing and looking towards the gloom that was barely visible beyond the dirty glass of the window, no doubt trying to make out the escape route. The oil lamp that they could see from their cell was lighted and illuminated most of the room. On the table was a stack of papers. The new warden sat down in his chair and directed Oleguer with a brief nod to stand before him and wait to be tortured or sentenced to death for trying to escape from a prison of His Majesty the mad King Ferran.

"You've been here for twelve years."

"Yes, my lord."

"Longer than anyone else."

"Yes, my lord."

As if he were alone, the warden picked up a stack of papers and looked at one of them. That gave Oleguer time to try and take his mind off his fear by thinking about the little workshop in Markkleeberg and the first, smallish organ that he had made, under Master Saltor's protection, for the private wing of the school of Saint Thomas in the populous city of Leipzig, only a few leagues from Markkleeberg. And then the longing had begun, not for Barcelona, where he'd grown up, but for the more distant and indistinct landscape of Sau, the place of his birth. And he didn't rest until he'd sold the workshop for a good price, made a detour to avoid going through Vienna, and gone back to the lonely and silent mountains of the valley of Sau, to think and to meet Maria, whom fate, always hiding behind a tree, never showing its face, had reserved for him. When he took the position of organ master in Vic, Maria was already pregnant with his son and heir. Celia wasn't born until three years later, after he'd made the splendid organs of the University of Cervera and the Cathedral of Manresa. And now he had to say goodbye, my beloved Celia, to the only person still left to him, because escape and intent to escape are punished with being hanged by the neck until dead.

The warden too had gotten distracted, but by reading those papers. As if he'd forgotten about the criminal whom he had to punish. Suddenly he folded one of the papers, very carefully, raised his head and looked Oleguer in the face for the first time.

"Have you ever received a letter?"

"Never."

"Who is Celia Gaulter?"

"My daughter."

Then, he picked up the stack of papers and pushed them across the table towards the prisoner.

"They're all letters from your daughter. She writes very well."

His legs began to tremble. Finally, finally, dear Celia, so many letters in one day, how is it possible? And all of them opened. The warden explained that his daughter had been writing to him regularly once a month and explaining everything that was going on, including the birth of his grandchildren.

"Grandchildren?"

"You didn't know about that?"

The warden gestured to him that he could keep the pile of letters. He didn't know whether to faint right there or wait to go back to the cell and do it. The warden, almost as if he were apologizing, said, "I don't know why they haven't given them to you, but she's been writing for years." And he couldn't keep from adding, "It seems that I know your daughter better than you do."

And with a nod of his head he indicated that Oleguer could go back to the filth of his cell, with the rats and the cockroaches. But with the letters. He could hardly walk, but he held the object of his delight tight in his hands. He didn't faint. The thin and sober warden must have ordered the jailer to put a light next to the door of the cell in case he wanted to read some of the missives before dawn. When he entered the cell, he sat down on his pallet, breathing heavily, both hands clasping the fat heap of letters.

"What did they do to you?" Faner whispered. But Oleguer didn't have the breath to answer. He was too agitated.

"Did they say anything about us?" Anxiously, Tonet.

Then he became aware of their presence. It irritated him to have those two pests there, keeping him from being alone with Celia, child, and me telling Massip that you didn't write to me. Poor Massip, who's been dead for years.

By the faint light of the fixture unwillingly hung by the toothless jailer, he was able to read the first letter, which said, My father, how are you? Tell me what you need, because Bertrana's sister-in-law told me she knows a man whose brother is serving in a company somewhere there, and he'll try and help us however he can. I miss you, Father, it said; but he couldn't read anything more because his eyes were filling with tears and those sweet letters were getting blurry. Faner and Tonet were leaning over him, whispering, alarmed, What the hell's wrong? Is it the death sentence? And he shook his head and cried, hardly able to believe that his daughter had written him so many letters. Grandchildren. He had grandchildren. And he cried some more. Tonet and Faner looked at one another, confused. A minute later, the henchman came to take away the light and they were left in the silent dark.

"It's almost midnight," said Tonet a little while later.

He didn't answer. He had too much to do holding onto the pile of letters and thinking of his daughter's pearly eyes.

After a while Tonet repeated, "It's midnight." And then, energetically, "Let's go."

"I'm not coming."

"What?"

In the dark he handed them the key that he'd held onto for a dozen years.

"I'm not coming."

"But you..." Incredulous. "Don't you..." He didn't understand. "But you've waited years for..." Desperate. "Why, Oleguer? Why?"

"I have to read my daughter's letters. I'll escape some other day."

"But... If we get away, you can see her."

"I've been waiting for so long," he muttered to himself, so the others could hardly hear. And louder: "Letters are meant to be read. You can go without me."

"But it's your idea. If we use it now nobody else will be able to do it."

"I have things to do. Some other day." And with a touch of impatience: "Go on. Good luck."

They looked at one another, stricken. Tonet shrugged his shoulders and said to Faner, Let's go. And, almost angrily, he pointed at the body on the pallet cradling a pile of papers: The damp has finally rotted your brain.

"You should get going," he said, eager to be alone.

The two conspirators got out of the cell with the key and disappeared silently down the corridor, towards the door that led to the attic. When the faint sound of their furtive steps could no longer be heard, he made himself comfortable on the pallet, using his daughter's letters as a pillow. That night, for the first time in twelve years, he slept soundly.

TWO MINUTES

She blew out the smoke, satisfied. See? Nothing happened. Being unfaithful is easy: two minutes, bing bang, and you've committed adultery. No angels were going to descend blowing trumpets of doom, obviously. And this man she hardly knew had a body like a model's, from all that yogurt.

"Why's your stomach so flat?" She said it in a friendly way, now that they'd gotten to know one another.

"I get a lot of exercise. And you shouldn't smoke."

He exercises. He takes care of himself. Unlike Ricard and me. The time comes when you just let yourself go and stop worrying about looking good, because the other person doesn't even expect it.

"I have to go."

"Wait two minutes. Do you think I'm pretty?"

"I sure do," lied the yogurt man.

A world-class orgasm her first time out, even though Neus had warned her that if she ever did it, she'd be more afraid than excited. Afraid that Ricard would find out, afraid of committing a sin, afraid of who knows what, of having it show afterwards when she went out, yes, but not of an orgasm, no way. And look what happened, and with the appliance repairman, who was an athlete, very sweet and strong, an animal. Why should she be afraid? She didn't owe Ricard anything, they didn't love each other. But if this was the day he decided to come home at the wrong time? No, in twelve years he'd never done that.

"You know what? Maybe you should leave."

The man got right up and allowed the woman, who was lit up like a torch, to look him over. Poor thing, he thought, but hey, a screw in the middle of the morning is always nice. He pinched her cheek, for something to do, so she could keep looking at him, and started to put on his clothes.

"Here," she said.

And she paid him for the repair plus a huge tip. He thought, Should I write it on her forehead or what. But he decided to pretend he hadn't noticed and put the money in his pocket. He'd take Katty out to dinner.

"What's your name?" Still in bed, anxiously rubbing out the just-lit cigarette in the ashtray, yearning, resisting the impulse to say, Come every day and take a look at my washer. In response, he kissed his index finger and smiled, as he'd seen Cindy Crawford doing on the cover of an American magazine. Acting the tough guy, he left without looking back. He picked up his toolbox and opened the door, hoping that no one would come along and make him feel uncomfortable. He closed the door softly and thought for a moment about the unknown woman he'd left in a strange bed. He didn't feel sorry for her. Or for himself either: he supposed he could become a professional gigolo, but rejected the idea with an embarrassed smile. Out on the street, he lit the cigarette he'd been wanting for a long time, wondered where the hell he'd left the van, and went through his list of addresses to figure out the best route to make up for the lost time. He stepped off the curb just as a silent limousine was approaching. Some car, he thought. Inside the endless limousine was a snooty chauffeur, with a gray uniform and an unfriendly face, and far behind him an impressive dark woman, very dark, like Naomi Campbell. The would-be gigolo thought he'd be glad to go to her house and service all the washers that needed it.

The chauffeur with the crabby face had to slow down because a man with a cigarette in his mouth and a toolbox in his hand was right in the middle of the street, staring open-mouthed at his client.

"Where the hell are you going? Watch what you're doing!" he yelled angrily. Then he looked in the rearview mirror at the Queen of the May to make sure she hadn't heard him swear. No, she was in her own world. Or not, because she looked up and, without raising her voice, despite the distance and with the impressive authority that emanated naturally from her wealth and her beauty, she told him to stop at the corner where the jeweler's was, two hundred yards farther on, and wait for her there.

"I can't park there," he said as he confirmed that the guy with the cigarette was still looking at them, made smaller by the rearview mirror, with his mouth still open and a cloud of smoke around him. Well, looking at the car or at Srta. Blanca; nobody ever looked at him.

"Do it somehow. It'll just be a couple of minutes."

The Queen of the May had two minutes to go into the jeweler's, smile, brush off three clerks, insist that Sr. Laporte come out of his office, tell him she'd just acquired the Buzi, 102.3 carats, say she was leaving a photograph of the stone (I suppose you've heard about Buzi and Ezequiel, Sr. Laporte) and he should start thinking about a gold necklace worthy of holding that wonder of nature and sublime testament to the skill and sensitivity of its cutter, and she'd come back someday when she had time. And she'd still have twenty seconds.

"Two minutes," said Srta. Blanca as she got out of the car. The chauffeur decided to double park, because trying to get that dinosaur of a car into the space available was risky. He got out of the car and eagerly patted the pocket of his uniform; he was smoking too much. He lit the cigarrette almost passionately. He took in the abundant, endless smoke throught the hole left by his broken tooth and felt better. And, out of habit, he looked at his watch to see how long the two minutes she said she needed would take.

"No way. You have to drive on."

The chauffeur looked up and saw one of those traffic wardens whose job it is to tell people how to park.

"It'll only be two minutes," he said, as he took the second puff.

Nothing irritated her more than servants of millionaires who defended their bosses as if they were family. And especially today, with that big Norwegian truck unloading paintings in front of the Fundació, surrounded by an army of security guards with guns, like her, but without the moral superiority conferred by the city government. She tsk-ed and repeated, in the same tone, so you could see she was fed up with the whole thing:

"No way. You can't park here."

"What do you want me to do? Put it in my pocket?"

"That's your problem. Or I'll give you a ticket. It's up to you."

"So how about that truck?"

"It's making a delivery."

She watched as the flunkey thought about it, sucking hard on his cigarrette and looking at his watch as if searching for a solution.

"If she doesn't see me when she comes out, she'll give me hell."

"I already said that's your problem," she replied, looking disgusted. "Find a parking garage."

"Where do you think I'll find one for this thing?" He pointed at the limousine with the gesture used by fishermen to show off the big fish they've just caught. "Really, it'll only be two minutes."

To calm her increasing irritation, she took out her book and prepared to write a ticket.

"Fine, here we go."

And she went towards the front of the car to look at the license plate. The chauffeur, now looking even crabbier, threw down his half-smoked cigarette and got into the car. Without taking her eyes off the license plate, she heard the angry slam as he closed the door. Good, he got it, she thought. She stepped back to keep him from running her over and acted like she was going to solve some other problem. As she watched the ridiculous limousine drive away, she smelled the cigarette, still burning on the ground. She went into a doorway, looked around, made sure there were no robbers or mafiosi or art traffickers bothering the guards around the Norwegian truck, and decided there was no danger. She lit a cigarette with practiced hands and started smoking, careful to hide the crime with her body. A two-minute break. Four puffs later, a gorgeous dark-skinned woman came out of the jeweler's across the street and looked around indignantly. It looked to the traffic warden as if she were waiting for a taxi. That's her problem, she thought. And she kept puffing on the clandestine cigarette and thinking that Carles was acting more and more uninterested, maybe... No, because they say a woman can tell right away if a man's being unfaithful and I haven't noticed any signs. But the thought irritated her. Then she noticed the blue car. Parked in an exit, for God's sake. She hated having to put out the half-smoked cigarette, but this guy wasn't going to get away without a ticket.

"God damn it," he said when he got close enough to see the traffic warden putting a ticket on his windshield. He came up, breathing hard. "Hey, it's only been two minutes," he complained.

"Nobody's ever been parked for more than two minutes," she said coldly. "You're blocking an exit."

"Damn it, I was..."

"Look, that's your problem. I'm just following the rules."

That was what really got him: saying it was his problem to run around all morning, make thirteen visits in two hours, spend a fortune on parking, leave the car in a spot for a minute, meet with a chatty client and, boom, a ticket. Shit.

"You know what I'm going to do about my problem?" said the potential heart attack as he grabbed the ticket. The cop stood waiting for the man to get it out of his system. Which he did by crumpling up the ticket and throwing it to the ground. Which is just what Carles would have done. Exactly. The man couldn't believe his ears when she said, with a smile:

"Fine. But I'll write you another ticket for littering."

That was too much, damn it all. He got in the car and, unconsciously, avoided slamming the door so the harpy wouldn't write him a ticket for making noise on the street less than three hundred yards from a hospital. He turned the key without worrying whether the cop was picking up the ticket and smoothing it out with her hand, or taking out her gun and pointing it at his goddam neck. He almost ran into a limo that was double parked in front of him. He put on his blinker and swung out and Shit, shit, shit. He had to slow down even more because there was a huge truck just... That's really a pisser, why don't they give him a ticket? Swearing under his breath, he stopped at the light, which was red. Mad about everything, he banged his hand on the steering wheel and the horn sounded, clear, ironic, and perfectly illegal.

Though she had good vision, most of her teeth, and legs that still worked just fine, what she couldn't do was break into a run in the middle of the crosswalk. So she thought, I don't care, make all the noise you want. And she looked defiantly at the nervous man who was putting one hand out the window of a blue car and drumming his fingers on the side as he lit a cigarette with the other hand. He was the one who'd honked, as if she couldn't see that the walk sign was still lit. Slow and steady wins the race.

She immediately forgot about the rude guy and started window shopping, which was what she liked to do when she walked home on that side of the street. Look at that dress. Not at my age. I'd like to find out what it costs, but I'm embarrassed. I can say it's for my niece. And what do they care, anyway? She saw a traffic cop writing something by a car and thought maybe she was giving somebody a ticket. If it weren't for my age, I would've gotten my driver's license long ago, she thought. And she kept walking so she could get home, because one thing she'd never done was smoke out on the street, it wasn't appropriate at her age. But another really nice dress caught her eye. No, she wouldn't dare wear that, at any age. They wear them really short these days. But it sure was pretty. She looked up and was startled; a shadow was reflected in the glass of the window. The shadow of a man with a dark beard who was singing the slave chorus from *Nabucco* very softly in a deep voice. The shadow thought, That old girl's scared. Right away he forgot about the old lady, who had continued on her way, mumbling about her fantasies, and concentrated on the window. Suggestive feminine apparel. The green dress wouldn't look good on his wife; she's too big in the waist. He corrected himself a little bitterly: her waist is getting bigger every day. Silvia could wear it, though. Everything looks good on her. He looked at the price. Good Lord.

Good Lord. He didn't know if he could indulge without his wife getting suspicious.

Regretfully, he turned away from the window. Then, to his annoyance, some uniformed guards motioned him off the sidewalk because workmen were unloading wooden containers from a truck. Paintings, he thought. They were taking them into the Fundació. It irritated him to have to step into the road because of the delivery. He should keep the exposition in mind. He should keep all kinds of things in mind, now that even his times with Silvia were starting to acquire a patina of boredom. And he began to sing very softly in his baritone voice a fragment from one of the songs from *Winterreise*, the one that said, *Eine Strasse muss ich gehen, / Die noch keiner ging zurück*,[1] which made him feel sad. In front of him, an impressive limousine came up fast and quiet out of nowhere and had to stop at a light thirty yards farther on. The man with the dark beard and the baritone voice took his key ring out of his pocket and with practiced fingers sorted out the right key before he got to the door. He began whistling his stair-climbing melody (the adagio from Dvořák's *American Quartet*), as he did every day of every year. He took in the Thursday smell of oven-baked rice and thought it was lucky his wife was such a good cook, if nothing else.

"Hi," he heard from the back of the apartment, "what are you doing home so early?"

"Hey," on his way down the hall, "did the guy come to fix the washer?"

---

1 "I must take a road from which no one returns."

DUST

*The spine of a book that is unopened and on the shelf speaks
with the desperate impotence of a prisoner, his eyes wide open,
who has been gagged by brigands.*
Gaston Laforgue

She'd wondered many times how many thousands of books there were in that house. But because she was on her best behavior as soon as she walked through the door, respectfully afraid to make a mistake and end up without a job, she'd never dared to ask Sr. Adrià that question. She just did what she'd been told: Monday, Wednesday and Friday, fill out cards in her careful handwriting. And Tuesday and Thursday, dust, because a layer of dust on a book is a sign of disrespect and carelessness. She started out doing it with a damp cloth, but the spines were black from years of neglect and the water made a dark paste that was even worse. So Tere told her it would be better to use the vacuum cleaner or, if that didn't work, an old-fashioned feather duster. She ended up with the old-fashioned method because it didn't even occur to her to ask Sr. Adrià if he had a vacuum cleaner. The books she was cleaning now had a good layer of dust on them, which she was trying to get rid of before he noticed it.

Sr. Adrià was a mystery. Maybe a millionaire, certainly a loner. He never went out, and he was always reading, going through books, writing cards or going over them, or unpacking, with obvious relish, boxes of new acquisitions, most of them old, worn books, some of them very old. He was obsessed with books. Toni was obsessed with sex, but Sr. Adrià was obsessed with books. Today, a dusting day, she'd end up exhausted, with her nose and her throat dried out and the taste of dust in her mouth, because in that house the bookshelves went on and on and the dust stuck to everything.

She felt him behind her as he turned a page of the book on the lectern, and she thought it was impossible for anybody to spend his life like that: people have to move, breathe fresh air, talk to other people, go out to eat, whatever. He didn't.

Victoria got down off the ladder she'd had to climb to do ORIENTAL POETRY. Out of the corner of her eye, she thought she could see Sr. Adrià watching her. When she checked to be sure, he was already deep in a book.

On the first day, when he opened the door with the lack of interest he showed for everything that wasn't a book, he asked how old she was. Victoria told him twenty and thought he would send her away because she was too young. And she needed the work because they were supposed to get married next fall. Age wasn't a problem, or lack of experience. Almost having gone to library school surely hadn't helped. She knew that what had made Sr. Adrià decide had been the delicate way the girl took the book that he handed her by surprise: she took it delicately, almost lovingly, just as Elisa picked up the embroidery box when she found out about the death of her lover in *Elisa Grant* by Ballys (Pittsburg, 1883). And on top of that, it turned out that she had beautiful handwriting. It was a good idea to get help because I can't keep up with things alone.

Today I'll do *Voyage d'hiver* (Lyon, 1902). Gaston Laforgue is rather pedantic and grandiloquent, but I've gotten six cards out of him. One very nice one about the nature of art. But he didn't understand anything about the life of Schubert. And, starting tomorrow, the complete works of Dario Longo (author's edition, Trieste, 1932), which promised some surprises, as he had seen when he used the letter opener on it the day before yesterday. I shouldn't have told her to do ORIENTAL POETRY because she's distracting me.

I should have sent her to CENTRAL EUROPEAN MORALISTS, 18th–19th cent., which needs cleaning just as badly.

Because she'd left a rag on top of the *fu* books from the Han dynasty, Victoria had to go back up the ladder, and Sr. Adrià found that the girl's buttocks were in his range of vision and figured they were what he imagined Adromache's buttocks must be like in the Cambridge edition: generous and discreet at the same time. She's finally leaving, he sighed to himself, and concentrated on his reading as Victoria went out of the reading room with the bucket, the rags, the duster, the ladder and Adromache's buttocks, in silence, and she could see that he was still involved with that thing about Schubert and she went down the hall full of books thinking, There's no way, no way: a few days ago he was eagerly reading a philological dictionary of Italian, and before that he finished *The Emotions and the Will* by Alexander Bain, which left him looking dazed for a couple of days. Who's Bain? she said. What the hell are you talking about, answered Toni, who got irritated when Victoria talked about work when there was nothing else to do. As far as he was concerned, Sr. Adrià was crazy, period. And Victoria held her tongue because she was beginning to accept that it was getting harder and harder to connect with Toni. Because the perfect Toni would have the education, the taste for culture, the discretion and the intellectual curiosity that Sr. Adrià had. Why was Toni so different? She didn't know how to answer that question. Or how to explain why in that house there was nothing by Magris, García Márquez, Goethe, Pedrolo, Gaarder or Mann. Why did Sr. Adrià read Ludwig Tieck (*Kaiser Octavian*), Giuseppe Spalletti (*Saggio sopra la bellezza*) or Jacob de Montfleury (*L'école des jaloux*)? Why did he collect sentences from those authors and he'd never even bought a single Faulkner? One day she copied out a few titles at random to find out if they had them in the library, and of course they didn't. Tere herself, all the years she'd worked there, had never heard of them. Ever.

And tea. On top of the books, tea. He drank six or seven cups a day. He drank green tea because, according to him, it relaxed the body and kept the mind alert. What she didn't know was that Sr.

Adrià was a vegetarian, as long as it didn't interfere with reading. There was no way she could know that; it was enough to know that he was clean, he paid well, at Christmas he paid her double, he never scolded her and he talked very little, as if he were aware that at his age he didn't have much time to waste. Never anything out of line. Ever. The perfect man, even if he was thirty years older.

Now the perfect man had taken out the magnifying glass and was looking at a sepia photograph in which the unfortunate author of the biography and some other people were being immortalized next to Schubert's tomb. With the magnifying glass he examined the inscription at the base of the monument. SEINEM ANDENKEN DER WI... It was impossible to read because the right leg of a smirking Laforgue hid the rest of the inscription. It upset him to think that the person in the way was keeping him from reading a text he'd never, ever, be able to finish. He turned the page: in the next illustration Laforgue, with his sepia smile, was pointing to the building where the composer had died. The unpaved street was muddy and the sky looked leaden. Sr. Adrià left the illustrations and said, Victoria, bring me some tea, and Victoria, from TRAVEL BOOKS, EUROPE, said, Yes, sir.

"Hours and hours shut up in an apartment with a man," Toni had said, one day when he was being particularly hard to take. Offended, she had answered that Sr. Adrià was a gentleman, and she had said nothing about those enigmatic glances that sometimes landed on her buttocks, because she was convinced, and that's why she admired him, that Sr. Adrià was an angel who was above human problems. If Toni had known about those glances, he would have gotten furious and tried to get into a fight with Sr. Adrià. Toni did look her over, from top to bottom, and actually his desire flattered her and sometimes she imagined it was Sr. Adrià who was doing it. Why couldn't Toni think about other things? Why couldn't he get around to reading a book sometime? In Toni's house, the only actual book was the phone book (2 vols.). From one extreme to the other, she thought. Because never having read a book sometimes seemed impossible to her. But nothing was impossible for Toni.

Except getting around to telling her what he'd done the last three Monday afternoons.

"Seventeen thousand five hundred fifty-two with this Schwartz that I just received and haven't catalogued yet," answered Sr. Adrià, hiding a touch of pride.

"You have more than the local library."

"Yes." And he gave her the week's wages with a gesture just like that of Phiné when he pays the traitor at the end of Verjat's *Les mérovingiens* (Lyon, 1899).

"And they're not the same. They're different kinds of books."

"Yes." He looked at her with a touch of reticence, with the cross-eyed gaze of the traitor (Verjat, *ibid.*), wanting the fog to lift because the first pre-cataloguing look at *Die Natur von der Klang* by a certain Klement Schwartz (Leipzig, 1714) awaited him. But Victoria asked a couple of other questions, which he answered, to put an end to things, with Maybe I'll explain it to you someday, and she disappeared down the stairs, her eyes bright like Raquel's in *Raquel* by Felip Cornudella (Barcelona, 1888), half embarrassed, half liberated. Schwartz's book was a treatise on the sounds of nature and musical instruments, from which he imagined that he could get a lot of cards, as usually happened with works halfway between scientific studies and poetic appreciations of the world. Once he had it in his hands, he realized that, half stuck to the inside cover, there was a very worn bookmark, a leather one, that was still a kind of yellow color and was decorated with the embossed figure of a fantastic and unrecognizable animal. He noted carefully in the incident book what book he'd taken it from, and forgot to deposit it in the objects case next to sixteen other bookmarks, dozens of dedications, folded papers with profound thoughts from anonymous readers (two of which had been worthy of cards), shopping lists, bills, and his favorite of all the documents imprisoned, like a sudden death, between the pages of a half-read book: a letter written in Yiddish, dating from the spring of '29 in Warsaw, in which Moishe Lodzer, a jeweler, communicated to the recipient his happiness and that of his wife at the engagement of their only son Josef, recently graduated from medical school, to

Miriam Levi of the Levis of Ierussalimskaia Street, and his prediction of happiness, prosperity and long life for the new couple. With almost liturgical respect for his beloved objects, Sr. Adrià passed a loving hand over the case, sighed, and initiated the first contact with Schwartz's book.

As she went down the stairs, Victoria congratulated herself on having been able to broach that subject. She'd been practicing for days: why don't you have anything by Balzac or Oller or Green? Why don't you have Foix or Hardy but you have De la Tapinerie, Laforgue, Triclinis and Schulz? That's how the conversation would begin. From there, he'd diverted her with the number of books and then, though he resisted, they'd gotten back to the nature of those books. But it was one of his laconic days and the conversation didn't flow. She dared to ask Sr. Adrià, Why do you buy books *like that?*

"What's wrong with them?"

"They're weird. They're..." And she let the stigmatizing adjective slip out: "unknown."

When they'd gotten to that point, Sr. Adrià opened the door of the apartment and waited impatiently for the buttocks of Andromache from the Cambridge edition to step onto the landing.

"Maybe I'll explain it to you someday," he said as she was descending, posing as Raquel for a few steps. When Victoria turned, hopeful, the door had already silently closed.

For a few days Victoria thought that Sr. Adrià would never explain the why of those books, and that made her frustrated, she who considered herself to be somewhat cultured, with fairly good English and a little French and a high pass on the college entrance exam. In any case, when she left work, she made a point to forget all about Sr. Adrià, since the thing she really wanted to find out was why Toni was at Lourdes's house every Monday, if according to him he didn't even know her, and how Lourdes, who claimed to be her friend, could do something like that to her. If anything was going on, which she couldn't be sure of. Or why her mother kept getting sadder and sadder. Sr. Adrià could go to hell, when she wasn't there. But she thought about him.

Six hundred twelve books later, Victoria was able to verify that Sr. Adrià had learned to be even stingier with words, and he didn't mention the conversation on the landing even once, and she admired him more and loved him in an open but intangible way. They had begun, with various quotes, some three or four thousand new cards, which he went over patiently on Saturday mornings as if he intended to memorize them. Saturday and Sunday were his favorite days because he was alone in the house, without Victoria's unpredictable presence. During this period of books, she, making an effort to get to know him better, had tried to find out how long it had been since the last time he went to the movies or the theater, how long it had been since he was in a bar, and important things like that. As a result, she was slipping a few points in his ranking. And because they didn't talk, Sr. Adrià had no way of knowing that Victoria's wedding had been postponed a couple of times: the first time because the explanations for the presence of Lourdes in Toni's house hadn't been satisfactory at all and the second, once they'd made up, because of her mother's sudden death. In fact, because of not knowing, Sr. Adrià didn't even know that Victoria had a boyfriend. But now he looked more insistently at Andromache's buttocks and had begun to notice, with surprise, Ariadne's breasts. Victoria had a prominent and well-structured bust, which he'd always ignored. But all that dust, all that going up ladders next to Sr. Adrià, all those cards, all that leaning over the paragraph he was pointing out with his finger, had ended up making Ariadne's breasts available for observation, and he imagined that he was Ponquiello about to caress the torso of the shepherdess Fida in *Pastorale* by Campdessus (Anvers, 1902).

One stifling day, Sr. Adrià fell ill. Sr. Adrià, in bed, in pink pajamas. This was certainly a novelty. He almost seemed to be a different man, except that he had five or six books spread out on his wide bachelor's bed. Had his beard gotten whiter? Maybe it was because of the light. Sr. Adrià invited her to sit on the side of the bed, because now there would be time to do cards. And he stuck out his arm for a few seconds, in silence, and then said, Don't get too close, I don't want you to catch anything. Just like Toni, she thought, the day he had a little cold he spent the whole afternoon telling her to get in bed with him, to help him warm up because he was freezing.

She could only remember one time she'd felt sick at Sr. Adrià's house. She was up on the tall ladder, dusting BALTIC NOVEL, 19th cent., and thinking that what connected her to Sr. Adrià was an intangible link. This moved her so much that her hand froze above the spine of a little book by Lautanias and she was overcome with dizziness. Sr. Adrià, who officially was reading *Cobra* by Marcel Gibert (Montreal, 1920), was observant enough to notice the girl's hesitation and to keep her from falling, practically by grabbing her. He made her lie down on the sofa, fixed her tea, and ordered her to take a taxi and not come back until the next day. In fact, the fainting had been produced not by the discovery of an invisible link between two noble souls, but by getting her period all of a sudden. She spent two days in bed with a hot water bottle on her stomach, and Toni didn't even drop by because he said she looked so weak that it killed him, he couldn't take things like that. In fact, he had tickets to a basketball final. He went with Lourdes, I think. What a difference: Toni didn't have pink pajamas. He didn't wear pajamas.

"Do you know why?" asked Sr. Adrià from inside his pink pajamas, taking up the conversation that had foundered on the landing six hundred and twelve books ago.

"No. I have no idea."

"Because I'm searching for wisdom... Because wisdom is shy and it likes to throw up smokescreens so people will leave it in peace. I pursue the unknown wisdom that always hides..."

"Where?"

He had fallen silent, his mouth open. For at that moment, laid low by fever, he had become aware of Victoria's real presence, as if a goddess had been sitting on the side of his bed for the last two centuries. And he started thinking she was beautiful, because her eyes had sparkled with curiosity as intensely as if they were well-cut diamonds. Sitting on the bed, her head bent towards him, her body turned sideways, emphasizing her splendid bust and the curve of her hips. He'd read over and over that there's an age at which everything comes together, when life seems pleased with you and all things enhance your beauty, for example in Guinizzelli's song in *Il ragno e la farfalla* (Milan, 1800). Victoria was at that age. Sr. Adrià tried to concentrate.

"In apparent mediocrity. Look."

He picked up one of the books on the bed and she, reacting professionally, couldn't help but notice that there was a dark patina of ancient dust on the front cover. It was *Pauvre Dido* by Abbé Renouaud.

"An epico-lyric poem made up of three thousand alexandrines."

"Is it good?"

"It's terrible." He opened it thoughtfully. "No matter how you look at it, it's awful."

"So why do you waste your time reading it?"

"And what's a good use of time, do you think? Going to the movies with your boyfriend?"

He said the thing about her boyfriend for rhythmic reasons, so as not to end the question too abruptly, not because he thought that a virgin like Andromache was interested in sexual matters. And he heard himself say, without meaning to: "Because you have a boyfriend, right?"

"Yes, sure."

So what did you think? That Ariadne wandered through the world alone, desolate, virginal, trembling at the memory of Theseus?

"Going to the movies with your boyfriend is a good use of time for you?"

"I don't know. But you said that *Pauvre Dido* is a terrible poem..."

"Worse than terrible. But I didn't say that I'm wasting my time by reading it. What's your boyfriend's name?"

"Toni. He's an EMT, an emergency medical technician."

Envy has changed the world; it has moved crowns from one head to another and taken heads from bodies. They say that, at bottom, Macbeth and his wife were moved not by ambition but by envy. Envy has made the rich unhappy, the poor wicked and the apathetic sinful. Envy has stirred up the basest passions and has affected every human activity, as demonstrated by Saint Alonso Rodriguez S.J. and documented in *Leven, doorluchtige Denghden ende Godturchtige Offeninghen von Alphonsus Rodriguez* by L. Jacobi S.J. (Antwerp, 1659). Despite these recorded precedents, for the first time in his life Sr. Adrià felt envy. Envy that was dark, hard, twisted, acid, cruel, bitter – the same adjectives that Clemenceau used to describe Virginie's rage in *Terre de Feu* (Orleans, 1922) when he discovers that the boat with Colette on board has just left. Envy because when Toni caressed his Dido from top to bottom, his fingers came away, in the words of Anuat Ibn Al Bakkar (*Trois gazelles*, Paris, 1858), filled with dahlias and scented roses. He too could go over poor Dido from top to bottom as many times as he wanted. But his fingers came away dark, blackened by the accumulated dust. And Sr. Adrià wished to be Toni the EMT.

He concentrated on making an effort. For the moment, he had to set aside that new feeling (new feeling?, Marta had wondered in *Les gavines del port* by Bartomeu Cardús, Reus, 1881, when she found the criminal hole in the net she was repairing) because the conversation was about something else and between his discovery and her body there was an unbridgeable thirty-year gap. It helped him a great deal to think of the words of T.S. Taylor, who affirmed that thirty years is the exact span of ridicule. It helped him to think of their two bodies nude and to imagine her laughing at his old age. And he came out with:

"I read *Pauvre Dido* and every now and again I find in it a thought that can be of use to humanity."

"And you write it on a card."

"And I write it on a card, or you do. For example..." He opened the book and flipped past many pages until he came to the one he wanted: "I'm translating," he warned, and cleared his throat, "'I love you so that I want to marry you, oh, queen,' said the prince, 'and if you do not wish it, I will cleave your teeth with my fist and your liver with my knife. And if anything is left of you, oh, beloved, I will wage war on you unto death.' Because you know, oh, human, that between love and hate there is the thinnest of barriers, as delicate as skin. And so Dido, who already knew this, lighted the pyre and plunged the knife into her stomach."

A few seconds of silence. Regretful, Sr. Adrià: "I didn't know how to translate it into alexandrines..." And more energetically: "The unknown wisdom of this fragment that everyone knows, because it's based on the Aeneid, doesn't lie in bringing to life poor Dido, desperate because Aeneas has left her, but in the hidden 'who already knew this'. Dido, the new Ariadne, is eternally deceived, because the fate of a good-hearted woman is to allow herself to be taken in by masculine tricks. Do you understand?"

"No."

And they were quiet for a space of five pages, the girl with her mouth open. Until she shook her head skeptically.

"I can't believe it."

"You can't believe what?"

"That you spend your fortune looking for phrases like 'which she already knew'. Sometimes it's more educational and fun to go to the movies."

"With your boyfriend."

"It's more useful to watch TV than to look for a 'which she already knew' in a book five-hundred pages long."

They were silent again. How could it be that he hadn't noticed what a pretty woman Victoria was until then? Now, exasperated as she was, she reminded him again of sad Andromache. More silence. Eetion's daughter took a breath and he dreamed that now he would declare his love for her.

"And also," Victoria said, almost as a rebuke, "you say the books you have are mediocre."

"Most of them. And unknown. And it's possible that no one has ever taken a careful look at them in search of great truths. Somebody has to do it."

Hector's beautiful wife stood up and smoothed her librarian's smock with a very feminine gesture and his heart leapt for the first time. She, with her hands on her hips, a little defiantly:

"What, exactly, is unknown wisdom?"

"Perhaps it's something you can't yet understand."

Andromache didn't back down; she looked at Pyrros with queenly pride and said, imprudently:

"Looking for unknown wisdom isn't everything."

The sick man was taken aback. Did she dare to contradict him? Sure of herself, she continued:

"You read these books because you're sad that no one's ever going to read them. Forgetting and forgotten people make you sad."

He said nothing. Andromache had pulled his great secret from him as easily as Belisario had torn the heart from his enemy in *Oro en rama* by Pérez Jaramillo (Buenos Aires, 1931).

"You want to bring them back to life by reading."

And without waiting for him to react, she said she was going to make tea and left the room. Instinctively, Sr. Adrià patted his chest to see if he still had his heart. Resignedly, he observed that when Andromache left, Troy went, inevitably, dark.

In the kitchen, she let the water heat up little by little as she thought about snippets of the conversation and the many thoughts that stayed with her more every day and furrowed, in a still invisible way, the God-given softness and texture of her young skin, which Toni had so far failed to notice. Some far-off words reached her, like the echo of Roland's distant horn:

"And style, do you hear?"

It was Sr. Adrià calling her, from the other side of the mountains, his voice hoarse because of his sore throat. She went to the room, a little rattled. For the first time, she noticed almost physically that, down the hall, through French Theater, 18th cent., she was getting nearer to his room because he was pulling on the ethereal thread that united them, like Theseus on his way back to Ariadne's haven after having slain the minotaur.

"Why style?" And in the sick man's bedroom the light went on again.

"I said it's a matter of style." He lifted his arm. "If a work is well written, the person who created is there in the words."

She didn't get the whole thing, but she was impressed by the image. As if he could read her mind, Sr. Adrià continued.

"It's not an image; it's reality. The soul is part of style. A well-written book cannot be forgotten. I love you."

"What did you say?"

"That an expression as banal as 'I love you' can form part of a soul if it's well placed within a sentence with purpose and style. See? I love you."

"Yes, but if you say it out of context..."

"Of course, if we take it out of context... Here, you say it."

"I love you."

And Sr. Adrià melted. Happiness paralyzed his blood, and a tremendous shock shook his memory to its very foundation. Sorrowful Andromache had declared her love for him. Then the whistle of the boiling water woke them up. She stood up and he made a gesture like that of Aeneas, meaning yes, she should put out the light, but somewhere else that was not in his heart.

Dido left the room a little disconcerted. He'd just said that he loved her, right?

Sr. Adrià, in bed, trying to decipher the sounds made by the goddess in the kitchen, regretted his cowardice, because he was incapable of grabbing her by the arm, pulling her into bed, undressing her and adoring her as Ignatius did to Laura in *Laura und Ignatius* by Lottar Martin Grass (Münster, 1888).

"It's not that I'm a coward. It's that she has a boyfriend."

He said it out loud, to see how it sounded, but he couldn't believe it.

"What?"

Victoria, silently, was coming into the room with the tray and the teapot of steaming beverage. And they weren't even in the Trojan winter but in high summer in Sr. Adrià's bedroom.

"Nothing. I haven't been sick in ten years."

Without realizing what she was doing, she put her hand to his forehead.

"You're burning up, Sr. Adrià."

"Do you know how to apply cool cloths to the forehead?"

That afternoon, Andromache didn't fill out cards or dust. She was the consolation of the afflicted, the sinner's refuge, paradise, the queen of the angels, the ivory tower, Saint Victoria, melancholy Ariadne, virgin of virgins, sad Andromache. She finally managed to get the new lover to drift off. As in a mystic revelation, as if in a celebration of the mysteries, as she cooled Sr. Adrià's burning forehead, Victoria like a new Nike, like a superior version of the worthy apprentice of *Der Zauberlehrling*, she felt herself to be gradually and firmly anointed, invested, consecrated to a new, profound and great power (cf. Ahnlund's *Skog*). Even her gaze changed, beautiful priestess invested with a new power.

" 'Gonzaga said to Isabel,' " said Victoria in a deep voice, officiating for the first time, " 'I take the fever from you and you offer up your suffering.' The novice looked at him sweetly and loved him even more.' "

Sr. Adrià suddenly opened his eyes, as if he wanted to be sure that it was Victoria who had uttered those words. A few lines of silence. She took it as a reproach and hastened to finish:

"*Forse che no* by Giuseppe Grilli, Naples, 1912."

Thirty-five new old books and some mysterious inquiries later, when his sore throat was a distant memory, Sr. Adrià knew that Toni was named Toni Demestre, was not an EMT but a nurses' aide, was twenty-five years old, often went whoring, and was fooling around with somebody named Lourdes Coelho. He knew all of this, but he wasn't sure he should explain it to Victoria. Spying was ugly, but making accusations was even uglier. So the only thing holding him back was aesthetics? And Victoria's happiness? Wasn't it more important to sacrifice his image as a discreet person if by doing so he was saving Andromache from the error of a bad love?

Now he heard her working in the hall and wondered if it was a good time to tell her everything he knew. But doubt made him hesitate. For the last few days he'd noticed a different, more powerful, brightness in her gaze. Twice when he'd gone in afterwards, he'd been able to confirm that Victoria had taken a book with her into the bathroom. Sr. Adrià dreamed that perhaps one day he would convert Andromache into a reader. Because emergencies take precedence over important things (cf. *Feliz Resolução* by António

Albes, Lisbon, 1957), Sr. Adrià asked himself again what he should do, tell her the truth about the EMT or pretend ignorance? Would he be brave enough to expose himself to the shame of Victoria's contempt for having been a snoop? Who'd told him to start spying on other people's lives? (That's what she'd say, imitating Felisa Graves, with her hands on her glorious hips.) Or maybe not, maybe she'd be eternally grateful to him for having opened her eyes. Or not. Or...

Sr. Adrià kept the secret file with information about Andromache in the big armoire, with the bedclothes, and he sailed, astonished, on an ocean of doubts. And I don't know whether to tell him I think it's strange that he's filled out only five cards in the last month, as if he no longer believed in what he was doing, as if we could allow *Örökkön-örökké* (Kálmán Szijj, Budapest, 1922) to be buried forever with no eyes tilling the furrows of its words (cf. *Letters and Papers* by T. S. Taylor Jr.) to rescue it from oblivion. He's distracted, preoccupied, as if he weren't interested in reading, and it pains me to see that the last thirty-five books he's bought have gotten no more than a distracted, apathetic glance, like that of Oliver Cage's Dorothy. What about Mazzarino, Spender, Caballero-Rincón, Seabra Pinto *et alteri*? What's he thinking about all day long, poor Sr. Adrià? Sometimes Victoria thought that the fevers of the sore throat had damaged his brain.

As if enlightened, like the anointed one she was, with the confidence inspired by knowing that what you do is just, Victoria climbed down from the ladder where she'd been cleaning AFRICAN POETRY and went into the study. She took Sr. Adrià gently by the arm, handed him the feather duster, whispered that he absolutely had to finish AFRICAN POETRY, in the hall, and sat down in the chair in front of the table in the study. Sr. Adrià looked at the feather duster, cast an attentive eye around him and left the room without saying anything. Andromache didn't pause, because she already knew what she had to do: Seabra Pinto's reflections on life in Coimbra between the wars would have more hidden secrets than William Spender's religious sonnets. She opened the book and realized that the spine, though it hadn't been on any shelf, was starting to attract dust. She made a grimace of disgust and wrote on a piece of paper that as soon as Sr. Adrià stuck his head in, she'd tell him that the books on the table had to be clean as well. She was only on page 3 when she found a good quote: "You are not alone, Coimbra, if the windows of your houses are opened every day, making the shutters bang happily against the walls." The happiness of the shutters, the happiness of the woman who opened her home to a new day in Coimbra... Victoria would have liked to be in the presence of Seabra Pinto as he was writing this thought; she had to be satisfied with reading it many years later, with the author dead. She read it again, with respect, she transcribed it onto a card and added "Coimbra." António Seabra Pinto, Lisbon, 1953. Immediately it occurred to her that it might be interesting, now that she'd broken off with Toni because putting up with him was getting harder and harder (he and Lourdes on the sofa in his house: that was the last straw), now that she had more time for herself, she could find the relationships, the indelible but ethereal links among the works: because Seabra Pinto's very direct, very latinate description (ibid.) had brought to mind "the port was covered with a thin patina of dust that only his sensitive heart was able to perceive" (cf. *Selbstaufopferung* by M. Haensch, Berlin, 1921).

In the hall, the dust from African Poetry made Sr. Adrià sneeze. He figured that he had a good hour of work ahead of him if he wanted to do a good job, book by book, spine by spine, and so keep Andromache's splendid library from falling into the disrespect and carelessness of oblivion.

EYES LIKE JEWELS

And Jaweh said to me: "I have made your forehead like the diamond, harder than the rock. Do not fear the sons of the house of Israel, do not tremble before them, for they are a caste of rebels."
Ezequiel

I tshak Mattes stood up solemnly and embraced the young man. Why such generosity? Why, the Lord be praised, has the venerable Maarten of Amsterdam chosen to favor me? Standing, speaking slowly in his cultured Yiddish so Baruch would understand him, he said, My son, may this Sabbath celebration be forever engraved on our memory. And the whole Mattes family, except for suspicious Chaim, said Amen. And the Lord heard their prayers and the family never forgot that Sabbath. Never did the honorable Itshak, or his wife Temerl, or their beautiful daughter Sarah, who was observing the newcomer with eyes like jewels, or her suspicious older brother Chaim, the scholar of the family, uninterested in the world of gems and devoted to the study of the Torah, or little Aaron and Daniel, still far from their bar mitzvah, or the vague uncles recently arrived from Warsaw, forget that Sabbath or the four days that followed it, the night that Itshak Mattes, raising his palms before Baruch Anslo, invited him to tell his story.

Baruch, after casting the eyes of his memory far back, began the narrative with a prologue. He said that his name was Josef Cohn and that he had undertaken that long winter journey because of the express desire of his venerable master, and that he wanted them to know that during the inclement weeks of the endless journey between Amsterdam and Lodz, despite the extreme difficulty of the conditions, not once would he have traded a single prayer of the Arvit in the imprecise light of dawn or one single Aixer Yotsar for the the small and innocent pleasures of a good straw pallet at an inn or a piece of cheese purchased in a village market.

(He is a holy man. So much the better.)

"My master," continued Baruch, "is called Maarten Claeszoon Sorgh and he is a famous diamond cutter in Amsterdam."

"May Adonai have him in his glory when his hour arrives, for he is a just man," said Itshak, and everyone but Chaim said Amen.

"One day I noticed that my venerable master seemed worried, bent over the account books that took up more of his time each day to the detriment of the gems, due to his gradual loss of sight. 'What is wrong, Master Maarten?' I said. And he answered that I was the only one who could carry out a task for him, but he dared not ask it of me. 'What task, Master Sorgh,' I protested, 'do you imagine I could not carry out for you?' The venerable master looked at me with his gray eyes full of wisdom and he said that he wanted to render homage to Master Itshak Mattes in the city of Lodz, in distant Poland."

"God in Heaven!" The tsaddik Itshak Mattes was once again impressed. "How can he have heard of me if I don't know him at all?"

"Your work is known in Amsterdam. Your cutting is much known and admired."

"Do you hear, Temerl?" Itshak, proud. "And I thought that the joy of my work was shared only by the diamond and myself in the moment that I release the fire within the stone by cutting it."

"I've always admired," said Baruch humbly, "the ability to find fire inside the ice of a diamond." In a lower voice, that made some of them shiver, he added, "the Lord has not granted me that gift."

There was a silence which each of them filled by giving private thanks to Elohim.

(Well, he has the hands of a diamond cutter, delicate, noble, with well-trimmed nails. How beautiful.)

Baruch went on after the devout silence. "He gave me three thousand Dutch florins, a horse, the advice that I take advantage of the voyage to meet and appreciate new people, places and languages, and the strict order to go east as far as Lodz, where he was sure I could stay for some time, protected by the hospitality of Master Itshak, before returning.

(May he never leave, may he never leave.)

Itshak Mattes stroked his beard, worried, and looked at Temerl, who said Yes with her eyes. He signaled his approval of the newcomer's petition.

"I left Amsterdam at the beginning of winter on a day that was sunny but bitterly cold. The ground was not snow-covered, but a freezing wind from the east, perhaps from where you are, kept Lambertus from making headway. In Utrecht, too like Amsterdam, I spent only one night, aware of my master's advice to learn about new people and countries and languages. My stay in Münster was slightly longer; they talk as we do but as if their mouths were full of straw, they're quieter and they're obsessed with..."

"They're papists in Münster." The icy voice of Chaim, the future rabbi, for the first time all evening.

"Yes, and I have to confess to having suffered some rejection for being one of the children of Israel. Münster was the first foreign city in which I had set foot in my twenty-three years of life."

(Twenty-three. And I am fifteen and my mother is already worrying.)

"I carried out some errands for the master and then, free of obligations, I shut myself up in a room in the inn to observe the Sabbath as best I could and to think about where I wanted the horse to take me the following day, all praise to Elohim."

A murmur of approval followed Baruch's last words. Only young Chaim, the devout, remained silent.

Baruch bolted the door and returned to the circle of light on the table. With nervous fingers, and aided by the stiletto that he used in the workshop to cut woolen cloth into pouches for the diamonds, he delicately began to undo the package. When he had it unwrapped, his mouth fell open. In the package there was a roll of canvas and two fat envelopes that, to the touch, contained only paper. Frantically, he unrolled the canvas, fingered the envelopes more carefully, and found the black bag of diamonds nowhere. There was no black bag with two diamonds inside. Damned be the mother of that bastard Maarten Sorgh; he sends me to Istanbul to return two diamonds as big as chickpeas and he doesn't put them in the package. Where are Buzi and Ezequiel? What is going on here?

Baruch, disoriented, looked out the window. Winter was dealing harshly with that part of Westphalia and the afternoon rain was just turning into snow that fell silently, covering all of Münster with a white carpet. He could barely make out the grim cages of the Anabaptists hanging from the tower of the church of St. Lambert.

He rolled the canvas back up, now examining it carefully. The bastard Maarten Sorgh was sending to his son in Istanbul the painting that had created such a stir last spring. Baruch set it aside and concentrated on the envelopes. One of them was blank and the other carried the name of the recipient, Jan Maartenszoon Sorgh, and the address in Galata, Istanbul. He brought this envelope close to the candle and spent a long time thinking about what his next step should be. After a while, he violated the seal with the stiletto. Inside, a thick fold of pages, all covered with dense writing. And no diamond camouflaged among the papers. Baruch began to read avidly to see if he could find the solution to the enigma. After the conventional introduction in which the miserable wretch Maarten Sorgh gave thanks to Elohim for all of his gifts, he asked his beloved son how things were in Istanbul and added that he was sending this letter via a special courier and by land because he wanted to prevent the information I am sending you, dear son, from being intercepted by the inspectors in the Ottoman ports, who, according to information provided by the Company to all those of us who have dealings with Turkey, are always on the lookout for secret information from our dealers. In the other envelope you have a complete list of suppliers, clients and owners of gems from Egypt to

Bulgaria, and as far north as the kingdom of Poland and the Baltic Sea. I cannot make use of it because I no longer have the energy to travel and these places are far from Amsterdam. But it could be valuable to you and help you to prosper. Use it prudently and let no one know of its existence. I have spent many years and a great deal of money collecting this information, and I want no one to profit by it but you. He who first knows the location of the river can become the owner of the water, says a Gentile proverb. Treat the list, son, as a precious good and make wise use of it.

I want you to know as well that a year ago, just as you were leaving Venice and starting out in Istanbul, the Imperial Diamond came into my hands. It comes from Dekkhan, was as big as a river stone and weighed 221 carats. The problem was that it was very irregular, too irregular, but I have never seen a diamond so transparent. I studied it for some weeks, but could not see its possibilities. My sight, son, is not what it once was. I showed it to Baruch Anslo, the carrier of this missive, who is an extraordinary cutter. He examined it and concluded that two stones could be made from it, in the form of brilliants. The Ottoman ambassador agreed, and Anslo split the Imperial. He got from it, as he had predicted, two stones of nearly a hundred carats and a few smaller stones. He did a magnificent job of cutting. The result was two magnificent brilliants; the smaller weighs ninety-six carats and is called Ezekiel, like the prophet, and the larger is one hundred seven and is named Buzi, after the prophet's father. They are a wonder: they bend the light of the sun in a thousand directions. When you receive them, via official maritime channels, return them in person on my behalf to the Sublime Portal. I have already been paid for my work, but do not reject an honorarium for your part in this, which will surely bring you fame and renown in Istanbul and beyond.

The carrier of this letter, Baruch Anslo, is a good cutter, as I have said. If he arrives at his destination, make use of him for a time, if you wish, but above all, do not trust him, for he has a beguiling way with words. Nor should you be deceived by his youthful appearance. He turned thirty this fall. He is twice as covetous, rapacious and cunning as he is good at cutting, which is why I did not trust the diamonds to him and decided to make him a target for possible thieves, as I hid from no one that Anslo would be the carrier of the diamonds. Moreover, he was beginning to look too insistently at your niece Rachel. If you have no interest in him, simply send him away.

Baruch Anslo left the half-read letter on the table. He had always considered himself cunning, but Maarten Sorgh had far outplayed him. Out loud he said, Filthy old bag of rat shit, may you hang forever on a Zeeland dune, the Lord be praised, and felt better. Then he continued reading the letter.

To fill the package with something that justifies the voyage, I am sending you a painting that is pretty but of no great value. I paid only five hundred florins for it. It is a portrait made of me last spring by Master Rembrandt Marmenszoon van Rijn, a painter who had his days of glory but has now fallen on hard times. Still, I recognize that he has made a pretty thing. The portrait took a great deal of work. The painter came to the house every morning, after Aixer Yotsar, at the time when I go over the client list and prepare my correspondence, as I do every day but the Sabbath, to take advantage of the morning light that Adonai deigns to grant us daily. Master Rembrandt chose my bedroom, which is now too large and, alas, too lonely, because it has the best light. I want you to keep the painting, dear son, not so much for its value, which is slight, but so that you will have, now that I know you will never return home because things are going well for you, a reminder of my old self and especially of the room in which your mother gave birth to you many years ago. This is the value it has, my son. Keep it with you and show it to your children and your children's children, that they should think of their poor grandmother. For you it will be a reminder of your origins, for there is no more painful death than the loss of memory.

Baruch Anslo put down the letter and opened up the painting. The portrait of the usurer Maarten going over his Devil's book, looking for the name of the fool to whom he could sell a diamond at three times the fair price, and entering in the profit column the money he took out of my salary for the little brilliant that inexplicably disappeared a year and a half ago.

He stood up and went to the fire. Baruch Anslo felt humiliated by the old man's cunning. After a long hesitation, he broke the other seal and carefully studied the secret lists. By midnight, when the city was white with cold, he had four ideas, but they still needed to be worked out.

He figured out the solution the next day when, though it was the Sabbath, he was out walking disguised as Benedictus Olson, stepping over the dirty snow near the episcopal palace, and Providence decreed that he should stop by a frost-damaged chestnut tree because, Providence be praised, the episcopal coach had stopped by the chestnut on its way into the city. His Excellency Monsignor Johann Christoph Götz, Defender of the Cross and Bishop of Münster, alighted, accompanied by his secretary. He wanted to take a look at the chestnut, whose health seemed to be a matter of concern to him. He patted the trunk, said something to the secretary, who nodded, and Baruch Benedictus saw them get back into the coach and go to the palace only a hundred yards away. Baruch Benedictus, on seeing His Excellency the Bishop, was stunned, his mouth agape. Now he could think of nothing but finding a good carpenter.

"As you can see, Monsignor," said Baruch, pointing to the easel covered by a sheet requisitioned from the hostel, "Master Rembrandt understood that in order to commemorate his celebrated conversion to Catholicism..."

"I was not aware he had converted."

"News, Monsignor," cut in Baruch Benedictus Anslo Olson, "is always slower than the truth." Before the other could praise the striking beauty of the aphorism, he went on. "The master decided to render homage to His Most Illustrious Excellency Monsignor Götz."

With studied emphasis he pulled on the sheet, and the episcopal secretary was able to gaze at the canvas, unrolled and displayed on a solid stand and surrounded by a frame that was at once austere and imposing. The monsignor opened his mouth, astonished. He looked at Baruch, looked once again at the canvas, and swallowed.

"But Rembrandt has never been here," he said admiringly. He pointed. "You, sir..."

"Gerrit van Loo, from Weesp," Baruch Benedictus Anslo Olson of Amsterdam continued humbly.

"... van Loo, do you know His Excellency?"

"I have that honor."

"But Rembrandt has never come to Münster!"

"I am his eyes, Monsignor." He lowered them humbly and went on. "I was in Münster the day that His Most Illustrious Excellency was enthroned, charged by my master with describing his features to him. When I returned to Amsterdam, I explained to Master van Rijn what His Excellency looked like, and he decided that, in order to avoid clumsy imperfections, he would make the figure small but surround it with an aura of wisdom and holiness."

"It is a perfect likeness." The episcopal secretary was still in awe.

"With this painting, Master Rembrandt wished to pay homage to all of the sages who, like His Excellency, spend the better part of each day, and even of the night, in the study of philosophy and holy theology, seeking guidance in ancient books full of wisdom." He raised a finger in conclusion. "You should know that Master Rembrandt has read Götz's entire *Tractatus Philosophicus*."

"Admirable." In an attack of sincerity, the secretary said, "I was incapable of doing it."

"Do you see?" insisted Baruch Benedictus Gerrit Anslo Olson van Loo. "The book that His Excellency is consulting in the painting is the *Summa Theologica* of Thomas Aquinas, Accordingly, the true protagonist of the canvas, along with His Excellency Bishop Götz, is the room itself and its atmosphere." He pointed an expert finger. "This is the reason that much of the painting is dark ochre, and the window, which admits the blazing light sent to us every day by Almighty God, stands out like a point of departure."

"It is truly beautiful."

"Do you see here, Your Reverence? These are the stairs coming down from a kind of ivory tower into the world in which we mortals busy ourselves far from wisdom."

"I should like to know why you are offering to sell us this painting if..."

"Once it was finished, my master said, Gerrit, my son, this painting has a destination. Go to His Excellency the Bishop of Münster and offer it to him as an homage to this city that has remained Catholic amid such turbulence."

"This is the first painting by Rembrandt that I've seen. Rubens is more talked about here."

"The experts say that Master van Rijn is the only one who knows how to paint air."

It was true. The air in the room, the space, the light, the contrast between dark and light. It was a marvel.

"This seems to me a most generous gesture on your master's part. Tell him that His Most Illustrious Excellency will accept the gift and the homage."

"Well... ," said Baruch Benedictus Gerrit Anslo Olson van Loo cautiously, "the master told me that I was to offer it to His Most Illustrious Excellency for five thousand Dutch florins, though it is worth three times that."

"Ah." The episcopal secretary looked again at the canvas, well placed by the window. "And what would happen if His Most Illustrious Excellency did not wish to pay this money?"

"With tears in his eyes he told me that if we did not reach an agreement, I should travel on to Rome and offer it to the Holy Father Alexander."

"At the same price?"

"At double the price."

The secretary went up to the painting to admire a detail. Then he stepped back a few paces and looked at the whole thing. His eyes shone like jewels.

"What title has your master given it?"

There was a slight hesitation, which Baruch covered up by clearing his throat.

"*The Philosopher*." He coughed a little more. "*The Philosopher Götz*," he finished after the false attack of coughing. "In homage to His Reverence and to his renown as a student of philosophy." For the first time, the secretary left off contemplating the painting and looked Baruch in the eye. Now he understood everything.

2

"In Münster, my friends, I understood the extent of the Catholic rage towards those of other confessions, even those of Christian sects. There are children here, so I cannot describe the horror of the tortures they inflicted a few years ago on the unredeemed Anabaptists, hanging them alive from hooks and condemning them to death from hunger, cold, exposure and thirst."

(Such delicacy. He is sparing us the details.)

"Death by starvation," from the cautious voice of Chaim, "in many places is reserved for liars and traitors. They are left to feed forever on their own falsehood."

"That is a great truth, noble Chaim," said Baruch. "But I was unable to trust the Gentiles and lived in a state of uncertainty. For that reason I had to hide my true faith and try to carry out my master's errands so that I could leave the city, which was dangerous to those who are not papists."

(How brave. His eyes are blue-gray-green.)

Baruch Anslo spent his last night in the holy city of Münster erasing his tracks. First he burned the letter from that disgusting old rat Maarten to his son. Then he hid in the most secret part of his body the list of clients and the names of the contacts so he would have access to the Sublime Portal. He made sure that no condemned paper, no fragment of wax, escaped the flames of the fireplace in his room. Then he made himself some credentials out of ink and his own imagination. By the time he was prepared, night had fallen. He wrapped himself up well and went out into the darkness, down the white streets, holding the reins of the faithful and silent Lambertus that the innkeeper had made ready.

3

"My horse is called Lambertus."

"That's no name for a horse." Chaim, distant and cold.

"An innocent joke of Master Maarten's. The animal knows no other name."

(Lambertus, what a pretty name for a horse. If someday I have a horse he will be called Lambertus and Chaim can be angry if he wants. Lambertus.)

"I've been lucky with Lambertus. He's a faithful and humble animal who has twice saved me from certain death."

(What!)

Itshak Mattes offered a challah to his guest, as if inviting him to rest a little or perhaps to make up for the danger to which he had exposed himself in carrying those precious documents. Baruch broke the braided bread tenderly. It seemed to Sarah that Baruch was not breaking the challah with his delicate hands but stroking its braids, and she shivered.

"Twice. Because in addition to helping me escape from thieves, one night, close to Scharmutelsee, which was completely iced over, I fainted in the saddle from cold and fatigue, and all by himself, stepping carefully to keep me from falling off, he took me in the dark to a post-house and neighed until they came out and helped me."

"What thieves? Why were they after you? Weren't you ever afraid?"

"I'm only afraid of the darkness of the tomb," he said in a brave voice. He smiled and looked around for something, and Temerl guessed that he needed a little wine to go with the challah. She served it to him herself.

He entered the square of Saint Paul's Cathedral at the agreed-upon time. As they had promised, on the north side of the building, by the cloister, a shadow was waiting, immobile, leaning against the wall. He tied Lambertus to a spindly tree and approached the shadow.

"Well?" he said by way of greeting.

"His Excellency was willing to pay only four thousand florins."

"In that case, you will have to give back the painting."

"No. He's kept it. He likes it."

"It's worth five thousand!"

"No. It's worth what a buyer gives for it."

"I will go to the authorities, Monsignor."

"Go ahead. Where will you begin? Where did you steal it from?"

"That is insulting. I work in the studio of..."

"Do you want the three thousand florins or not?"

"Didn't you say four?"

"Now it's three."

The shadow stretched out a hand with a full purse. Baruch Anslo took it nervously and opened it. By the cold brightness of the white snow, he estimated that there were perhaps two thousand five hundred florins in gold coins. A shot of rage ran up his spine. He smiled.

"It has been a pleasure to deal with you, Monsignor."

First he slipped the purse into his girdle, and then he took out the stiletto and thrust it, through layers and layers of clothing, into the episcopal secretary's stomach. It all happened so fast that when the monsignor was on the ground, darkening the snow around him, he had not lost the ironic smile with which he had handed over the purse containing two thousand florins to the swindled swindler. Aware that the man was still alive, Baruch Anslo took off his clothes. The secretary made a moan that turned into a death rattle.

"Don't bother to scream because I know you came alone."

"Call someone. I don't want to bleed to death. You can still get away."

"First give me the money."

The episcopal secretary said, Don't kill me, and fainted. Baruch Anslo finally found the purse. It was fuller than the other. It made him so furious that he stabbed the episcopal secretary in his noble gut once more. He left him convulsing against the wall of the cathedral. A few steps away, struck perhaps with compassion for such useless suffering, he went back to where his victim lay. With the stiletto he opened a sinister smile in his throat, and the monsignor, the swindler swindled by the swindled swindler, finally stopped trembling, infinitely weary.

Instead of taking the road for Frankfurt, which would lead him straight to the Danube, instead of turning onto the route which would have taken him to Istanbul, as he had mentioned two or three times to the innkeeper, Baruch turned the horse towards the rising sun, on the old road to Warendorf, in search of revenge. Goodbye, Rachel Sorgh. I'll find you again in Magdeburg or farther to the east, I'm sure.

When the sun came up over the snowy road, he stopped Lambertus and opened the monsignor's purse. That stinking thief had been good at milking the vanity of the most illustrious Bishop of Münster; in the pouch, in the form of a few heavy coins, was the equivalent of more than thirteen thousand gold florins. Never trust anyone.

4

"But what thieves?"

"It was after Münster."

"Please don't be so impatient, dear Temerl. You have to give him time to explain himself."

(As far as I'm concerned, he has all the time in the world.)

Baruch Anslo thanked Itshak Mattes for his assistance. He took a drink of wine and continued.

"After I'd carried out the errands, there was no reason to stay in a city so harsh to foreigners, and following my venerable master's instructions I went east, towards still distant Lodz."

(How well he speaks. He has a poet's mouth. And poetic eyes.)

"It is in Elohim that I place my trust. So when I met up with the thieves I was telling you about, in an inn outside of Magdeburg, it was the Lord's will that they did not find the little money I had on me and left me for dead."

He pointed to the scar on his left arm that he'd gotten in a canal in Amsterdam three years ago, and a pair of blue-green bottomless eyes filled with tears.

(If I'd been there to defend him or cry out for help...)

"Three cruel bandits." Baruch found the memory upsetting. "I took one of them down. But the other two ran off, and since I was wounded... But that wasn't the worst of it. When I was going through the forest that they call Schönenbaumgarten, a dense, dark place where the trees stand close together, those two wretches were waiting to get their revenge. I've made this journey unarmed, and I was at the mercy of their hatred."

(Oh, Lord God in heaven. And I was here, not even worried...)

"And then Lambertus saved me. Without my telling him to, he took off, leaving the road, and went right through the forest as if he'd known it all his life, and managed to leave them behind, We didn't get lost because he smelled the high road after a few hours. I never saw them again, those awful men."

(Whoever says Lambertus isn't a good name for a horse has no feelings at all.)

Lambertus raised his head. He seemed extremely fatigued, though Baruch had not pushed him. He snorted in the direction the post house. No doubt the odor of burning wood reminded him of a place to rest, away from the infinite snow of that white plain. The poor beast was sweating copiously despite the cold, and Baruch, perhaps with a bad conscience, patted him reassuringly on the neck.

He didn't see them until he dismounted. There were three of them and they came out of the inn menacingly. The one with the feather came up to Baruch as soon as he'd dismounted.

"Sir, we have orders to inspect all travelers on this road."

"May I know why, sergeant?"

"The murder of a high official of the Church."

"I'm coming from Bremen. Where did this terrible thing happen?"

"In Münster, five days ago. In any case, we have orders to go through everything. Wherever it comes from."

Baruch, very courteously, showed them his credentials as emissary from the kingdom of Denmark on his way to Leipzig, and asked the sergeant to have the deference not to search through the rest of the papers in the document pouch, to which the sergeant agreed, Because we're not looking for papers.

"And what is it you're looking for?"

"We're not authorized to reveal that to anyone."

"In that case, I'm at your disposition, gentlemen."

And they went through absolutely everything, the bastards. Everything meaning that they put him in a room, they made him tell his name (Peter Nielsen), birthplace (Alborg), profession (optician) and the reason for his journey (I'm sorry, but for obvious reasons I cannot say any more than I already have). Afterwards, amiably but firmly, they stripped him naked. He reminded them uselessly that he was an emissary of the kingdom of Denmark, and they went over every stitch of his stinking clothing, his pouch, his shoes, his blanket and Lambertus's saddlebags, and left him shaking with indignation and cold. When he had dressed, he demanded that the sergeant apologize to an emissary of the kingdom of Denmark on his way to Leipzig, but the sergeant and his soldiers had no time for games and paid him no mind. Besides, two more travelers had arrived. At the inn that night, they told him that his horse was unwell and he could change mounts.

Baruch said nothing but he slept with one eye open, listening from time to time to poor Lambertus neighing, and before it was light, ignoring the advice of the stableboy, he mounted Lambertus with the intention of following the sun. Below him, still in shadow, the famous city of Magdeburg. Lambertus, who was starting to urinate blood, now walked purely out of obedience. So when they arrived at the banks of the Elba, he dismounted, took off the saddle, and made the beast lie down on the grass. His breathing was so labored that it broke your heart, and it was clear that he was in unbearable pain.

"I hope you will forgive me, dear Lambertus," he whispered into his ear. And he severed his jugular with the stiletto. The animal shuddered harder than the episcopal secretary and his eyes became glassy. Without waiting for the death throes to end and after making sure that he was completely alone, Baruch opened the horse's gut with a precise motion. He thrust his hands into the stench spilling out of the intestines, and then farther, until he came to the stomach. All of the coins were there, bloody, filthy, but whole, offering their gold to Baruch. He left nothing behind. When he was picking out the last one, he thought he could feel a slight tremor in Lambertus's body. Goodbye, Lambertus, he said without turning around, as he left carrying the saddle.

He went on foot for a couple of days. On a road outside Mödkem, Baruch Benedictus Gerrit Peter Anslo Olson van Loo Nielsen bought a tall, nervous horse, which he baptized with the name of Lambertus, and pushed on to get away from those places where, involuntarily, he had left traces.

5

"After thirty-six days of traveling under fearful conditions, I finally arrived, Adonai be praised, at the end of my journey. Spread before my eyes, weary of so much winter, were the houses of the city of Lodz, and in one of them was the family to whom I was to bring my present."

(How could we be so lucky.)

"You are an honorable and well-known person, Reb Itshak. I had to ask only once and I was sent to the right house. The first person I saw... was sweet Sarah, who was standing on a mound of peat, looking out over the road."

(How nice he is. I could just eat him.)

"And here I am. Now you know everything about me."

Everyone was respectful of the silence that fell. Baruch himself broke it after taking a sip of that warm and welcoming wine.

"I don't want to disturb you," he announced. "With your permission, I'll prepare to return to Amsterdam as soon as I've recovered my strength."

(But what are you saying? You just got here.)

Silence. Itshak Mattes was thinking of the newcomer as a possible assistant to whom he could teach the secrets of the art of cutting, given that Chaim was distancing himself, drawn by study and prayer. Temerl was thinking, Poor young man, he must rest for as long as he wants and the voyage is dangerous. He can't leave until summer. Chaim was appraising Baruch's eyes, but silently. He was silent inside.

(Let him stay. Stay. Forever, Josef.)

At night, when everyone was asleep, Chaim Mattes shook him energetically by the shoulder. Young Baruch, half asleep, thought, This is it, Maarten has sent someone after me and I'm finished.

"Josef, wake up!"

It took a while for him to realize that it was suspicious Chaim, with a light in his hand. Baruch tried to sit up, his eyes wide with fright. Chaim, yes. He calmed down.

"What do you want? What is it?"

Chaim, with the flat of his hand, kept him down.

"Everything you said tonight was a lie."

"What?"

"No one in Amsterdam knows my father. That's impossible."

"He's on the list. And he certainly thinks it's possible."

"Pride and arrogance blind our eyes."

"You concentrate on the Torah and leave me in peace."

Chaim left the light on the nightstand. The chiaroscuro was reminiscent of Caravaggio and Rembrandt. Once again, he held Baruch down.

"Why have you come?"

"On the orders of my master."

Chaim opened his fist. Five gold florins. He left them on top of the nightstand.

"How is it that you're so rich? Your purse is full."

"What you're doing is an insult to your family's hospitality."

"What have you come to do?"

"For your own peace of mind, tell your father to find out... I don't know, if Itche Hertz in Warsaw buys second quality at the price of first."

"If I find out that you're trying to steal from my father, I'll kill you."

He gave him a seemingly affectionate slap on the cheek and left the room, with the candle. Baruch, in the dark, began to make plans.

Two rooms farther down, Sarah, in her dreams, recited the Aleinu transported with joy at Josef's existence and begged him not to leave, never to leave.

He had to wait for three days. On the fourth, Itshak Mattes, after shutting himself up with his son for hours in the workshop, left for Warsaw to look into the business of that Hertz. Baruch had to wait only until the suspicious son went to cheder to teach the boys the rudiments of the Mishnah, the reflections of the Gemara and the history of the people of God taught in the Torah. All praise to Elohim, because finally Chaim's eyes are no longer boring into my thoughts.

Baruch waited for the moment when Temerl was involved with preparing that night's borsch and turned his best smile onto Sarah.

"Why don't you show me the workshop?"

"When father isn't here, we can't go in."

Baruch put his hand on her back, made her tremble with emotion and said, But I'm here, and I'm a sort of big brother, right?

(Big brother, little brother, any kind of brother, Josef, I love you.)

"Yes."

"So?"

She let go of her last scruple and unhooked the key from behind the stove (a very clever place, he would never have figured it out all by himself), took the hand of her Theseus without knowing that she was Ariadne, and led him toward the dark labyrinth.

Shadows, darkness, stairs that went unbelievably far down, and, after a few turns, the distinctive smell of diamonds that only he was able to detect.

"I wonder if..." He shook his head, serious. "No, never mind, let it be."

(My love, what is it that you don't dare tell me? That you love another? That you're married?)

"No, what is it? I'm willing to..."

"Well, I was wondering if... if you'd like me to kiss you."

(The Lord be praised.)

"You're sure? Do you mean that...?"

"Yes, you're right, Sarah. Forgive my boldness."

"No, I mean..."

(Oh, yes, my love. Kiss me once and I'll kiss you a hundred times and feed off your indestructible love and you and I will live forever in a paradise where the rivers and streams run with milk and honey.)

"The facets of your eyes are very well cut, my love." He brought the light close to her. "And when the light shines on them, they sparkle as if they were jewels. I love you, Sarah."

Sarah, in response, stood on tiptoes and covered his mouth with a kiss inappropriate to her age but very exciting to Baruch. A thousand days later she let go of her Josef, and he told her, I've made a mistake: to compare your eyes with simple diamonds is to do them an injustice.

"I like your eyes too, Josef Cohn. And your hands."

"Where does your father keep the diamonds?"

"In a secret place. Why?"

"To compare them in front of a mirror. Next to your eyes, a diamond loses all its value."

"Do you really think my eyes are so pretty?"

"They're the most beautiful light I've ever dreamed of. You know, a diamond needs the sun to coax out the fire it has inside.

But your eyes..." In tears, Baruch confessed, "I didn't know there could be such beauty in the world."

Sarah, trembling, pushed aside the work table while Baruch held up the light at a prudent distance. Behind a tattered curtain hung from the wall, a cavity closed off by a solid wood door.

"The key isn't here. They usually keep it here but..."

Baruch brought the light close. It was a Larszoon lock.

"Too bad," he said out loud. When your father or your noble brother Chaim have returned, we'll ask them to let us try it.

When the happy and the careless were sound asleep and the house itself was resting, Baruch took the key from behind the stove, went into the depths of the workshop and stood before the Larszoon lock with a skeleton key and his stiletto. He opened the lock before the candle had burned down one finger-width. The door opened onto a storage space cut into the wall. To the side, some little boxes on shelves. He brought the candle up to them and the jewels and the diamonds multiplied in explosions of joy, like Baruch's eyes. He looked hard at one of the boxes. He brought the candle up to it and said in a low voice Those sons of bitches holy Itshak and his milksop son. Crystals that smelled of glass. Glass! A cheap copy that... Then he saw that there were more boxes behind, and he took a step inside with the candle. Behind him a soft sound, a little current of air, enough to blow out his candle. The door had closed and someone was working the Larszoon lock with a key and sealing the tomb of Baruch Benedictus Gerrit Peter Josef Anslo Olson van Loo Nielsen Cohn.

"You can eat your lies," he heard, muffled, from the other side of the heavy door, before he fainted from terror.

GOTTFRIED HEINRICH'S DREAM

It is music: it has come from a heart.
J.S.B.

At four in the afternoon the old man sat up in bed and said, Kaspar, son, where are you? B-flat, A, D-flat, B, C. The phrase had returned suddenly to his memory. Hearing how poor Gottfried played the clavier had always made him sad, very sad. He remembered Gottfried's gray eyes, open as if they wanted to flee from behind the notes strung together by his long, nervous hands. He imagined his unruly heart, which made him look at women with an anguish that more than once had made the old man tremble. And, especially, the disordered thoughts that forced him to live in constant mental chaos.

These things had made them both cry, he and his faithful Magdalena, when Dr. Müthel told them that Gottfried Heinrich wasn't all there; he would grow like other children, but they should expect no mental effort from him because he had no thoughts. Nevertheless, one day hope appeared, like a ray of bright light. They could see that the doctor was quite wrong: Gottfried did think. But it seemed that he thought with his heart and not his head. It was a cold day and very snowy, a day when his father was particularly tired on the way home from the Tomasschule, ready to blow up the entire Ineptitude Brigade en bloc. As he was walking the short distance to the house, he heard a strange stammering from the clavier and he found Gottfried seated, at the age of seven, imitating

79

his posture, leaning over the keyboard, his eyes vacant, playing a not very transparent version of *Contrapunctum VIII*, which he had been working on at the time, the child bent over the sounds, sweating, so transported that he wasn't even aware of his father's presence. No one had taught Gottfried the art of the keyboard, because nothing can be taught to a child without thought. His father, standing, silent, his wig in his hand and his mouth open, saw that his beloved Gottfried had thought, memory and will, because if he was able to reproduce something so difficult, he could think, remember and apply himself, God be praised. And the master wondered which school he should take him to the very next day. But, after several attempts, the complete failure of this initiative forced them to the bleak conclusion that Gottfried had thought, memory and will only for music; for everything else he was still what Dr. Müthel had told them: an idiot. And he always would be. But after the day of the *Contrapunctum*, Gottfried had his father's express permission to play the clavier, like all of his brothers and sisters. They often listened in silence, the older ones respectfully and the younger ones somewhat fearfully, to the wild improvisations that could go on for a long time bringing tears to Magdalena's eyes as she prayed silently and said, My poor son, my poor son, he has thoughts only for strange music.

On February 26, when they were celebrating Gottfried's sixteenth birthday, all of the siblings who were present asked him to improvise, and as he always did before he put his hands on an instrument, he raised his eyes and looked beseechingly at his father, his mouth open, showing, without realizing it, the hole where his tooth had been broken in a brawl two years ago in the lane that vomited mud and sewer water into the Pleisse, requesting a dispensation that his feeble head could not understand had been granted him forever. And the father had to nod his head so that blessed Gottfried could play with a tranquil spirit. The old man remembered that that day was especially difficult because Gottfried started out with an unusual theme, B-flat, A, D-flat, B, C, which raised protests from his siblings, which he silenced to see where it would go. Everyone understood that Gottfried's improvisations on this theme would lead him straight to hell. But out of pity for the emptiness in his head, they let him play for much of the afternoon, until Elizabeth, dear Liza, to distract him from that diabolical music, suggested that they go throw snowballs in Saint Thomas's square. B-flat, A, D-flat, B, C: a kind of phantasmagorical and unseemly version of the familiar theme, which took the form of BADESHC. Which meant nothing to anyone, except that in some strange and ancient language Badeshc was the occult name for Satan.

This theme and the music derived from it had come back into the old man's memory. That is why he sat up in bed, turned his useless eyes to the wall and murmured Kaspar, my son, Kaspar, don't you hear it?

"I hear nothing, master."

The boy shuddered. He'd fallen asleep, with the book open. The master had fallen asleep before he got to the end of the seventh chapter. And that treatise on the sounds of nature was so boring that the very memory of the pages he'd read had made him succumb as well.

"Has Gottfried come back?"

Kaspar woke up. He put, at the appropriate page, the piece of yellow leather with the embossed lion that the master always used as a bookmark, closed the book and left it on the bed table, next to the brownish medicine that was left in the glass. His recently awakened mind soon oriented itself.

"He's staying with the Altnikols until..."

"Until I die."

"Those were the arrangements you made."

Kaspar, alert, expected the master to react strangely. But he neither got upset nor let his body rest against the pillows. Instead, he flung aside the thin sheet and made as if to climb out of bed. Poor Kaspar, frightened, didn't know what to do.

"But, master... You can't..."

"I certainly can. I'm not dead yet. Where's my walking stick?"

"I don't know. I don't..." Disconcerted. "Your walking stick? You want your walking stick?"

"No one thought I would walk again. Have you thrown it away?"

"I can be your walking stick, master."

The old man agreed, admiring the quick response of the lad he called son and would have been glad to have as a son. Meanwhile, poor Kaspar was cursing his bad luck. The mistress had to be away until nighttime and they'd told him to respect the master's desires, however trivial.

"Take me to the organ."

Kaspar had to be the master's improvised staff. He could imagine the long faces of the family when they found out what had happened. But he was there to respect the master's wishes, however trivial.

They went through the family dining room and the clavier room to the door that led to the organ chamber.

"The key should be in the lock," the master said. And yes, it was. Breathing with difficulty from the effort, the master leaned against the wall and said to himself, Wall, blessed wall, you surely didn't expect that I would lean against you ever again.

"Do you want to go back to bed?" asked Kaspar hopefully.

"Absolutely not."

Once he had recovered from his fatigue, the master made some secret taps on the wall and, on the boy's arm, went into the organ room. As if he were seeing it: not an especially large instrument, with few registers, but mechanically very solid and dependable and amazingly pitch-perfect. Kaspar opened the shutters and the early July light fell on his appreciative eyes, passed indifferently over those of the master and lit up the keyboard of the organ and the Hausmann clavier, the master's favorite.

"The bellows, Kaspar."

The boy went to the bellows and opened the airway. He began to work the bellows and suddenly the theme appeared, B-flat, A, D-flat, B, C, poor Gottfried's diabolical theme, which Kaspar couldn't know because he hadn't been born when it was heard for the only time within these walls. And then he was developing the theme for a good thirty measures of counterpoint and producing some strange, dissonant screeches, and sevenths and ninths without any logical or structural basis, just what the master said you weren't supposed to do, and no care taken with the voices, because the chords weren't complete. Oh no, now in the trumpet register, the most piercing one, a bitter melody and its fleeting, dissonant imitatio... Well, Kaspar refused to admit that it was a melody. He looked at the master and was surprised to see him smile.

The master was smiling because he was accepting Gottfried's dream and realizing that what his son was saying with those whistles was that he too existed, in his way; and he intuited vaguely that one day this might be music. He ended in an abrupt way, with a brief, impossible chord: C, D-flat, D, E-flat, E, F. When silence fell, he heard Kaspar stifling his sobs, his head against the rusty metallic plaque in front of him confirming that Olegarius Gualterius sauensis me fecit in Markkleeberg, Anno domini 1720. From his place by the bellows, Kaspar did not dare to look at the master's blind eyes.

"I haven't gone mad, Kaspar."

"What is that?"

"The dream of an innocent. And I'm making seven variations. I have them almost finished."

Kaspar thought he was inside a hellish nightmare. And he shuddered when the master, instead of asking, Take me to bed, I'm tired, said, Copy what you've heard, Kaspar, because we still have a lot to do.

"But that's not music!"

"Don't tell me you don't remember..."

He said it in a softly menacing tone, the most frightening one. Accustomed to obedience, Kaspar went to the desk, took out the pen, the ink and the staff paper, and began, with the ease conferred by his extraordinarily retentive memory, to write down that horror as if it were music.

"It sounds very ugly, master," he said when he saw that he had to repeat the twenty-seventh measure of the theme.

"It sounds the way it's meant to sound to the pure of heart."

Now he was quite sure that the master had gone mad. He sighed and finished the job with the return of the initial theme and that horrifying ending of C, D-flat, D, E-flat, E, F. He put down the pen, unable to keep from grimacing in disgust.

"I've finished, master."

"Now play it on the clavier."

Utterly insane. But because Kaspar had been brought up to obey and make music, he obeyed. But he didn't make music; he produced chilling, scandalous sounds, that not even the most mischievous children could imagine getting out of a clavier if left alone with one.

"F-sharp, G-sharp, A!" the master scolded.

"But it sounds even worse," he replied, as an excuse. "If we start in E-flat major ...."

His blind gaze lost in a future he could not know, he muttered something that he would never have dared to say, were it not for his beloved Gottfried.

"It doesn't matter where you start out. There is no tonic. Theme and development are just a mirage... There is unexpected music, always."

"And the dissonances?"

"The Lord has created them too." After pausing for a few seconds he put out his hand towards where Kaspar should be and, almost in a whisper, he confirmed the order: F-sharp, G-sharp, A...

And Kaspar did F-sharp, G-sharp, A, and the horrifying sounds were realized as the master had foreseen. Then the master started dictating, furiously, with the speed of a dying man who doesn't want to go without having left, like an anchor for memory, his last thought, a thought enlightened by his daring, a canonical counterpoint, with a perfect equilibrium among the fugued parts, starting from the madness of the initial theme. And based on this, six more variations, all based on the same... on the same lack of tonic, as if all notes had the same value and there were no such things as tonic, dominant, subdominant and sensible. Kaspar thought that he would go mad, but he obeyed and copied with absolute fidelity what the master dictated. After two hours, the master was pale and sweating with the enormous effort he had made. Then, without moving from where he was, gripping the sides of the table, he croaked, Now, Kaspar, I'll play the whole thing on the organ. Listen as you work the bellows in case you've missed something.

"I haven't made any mistakes, master." Kaspar said this without boasting; he simply made music well, always. "If there is a mistake, the one who…"

"The thoughts are not wrong, Kaspar." He cut him off somewhat rudely. "Try to be generous. If you don't, you'll never understand."

The master played the theme and the various counterpoints, and the walls of the house wept because they were unaccustomed to hearing, in that home, such uncontrolled moaning.

When he had finished, the master was downcast and visibly fatigued, but with his attention fixed on the realization of his son's dream. His blind eyes lit up and he looked towards the bellows.

"Can you keep a secret, Kaspar?"

"Yes, master."

"Bring the pen and paper."

The boy obeyed rapidly.

Pointing to him as if he could see him: "Write down the title of the piece." He looked away, as if searching the limits of his memory, and recited, "Counterpoint on a Theme by Gottfried Heinrich Bach." He waited, impatient. "Do you have it?"

"Yes, master."

"I like the organ better than the clavier. Tomorrow you'll make me a version for the lute. Do you hear, Kaspar?"

"Yes, master, for the lute." He swallowed.

"Did you like it?"

"No, master, not at all."

For the second time that day, the old man smiled.

"I do. Put my name on it."

"You want to sign it?" Poor Kasper was shocked once again. "That?"

"Yes, that, Kaspar."

In a shaky hand, Kaspar wrote out the signature that his master rarely asked of him: Johannes Sebastian Bach fecit.

"Thank you, lad." The old man sighed, at the limit of his strength. "Now you have to take me right to bed. And the thing we've written... hide it for now." He sighed. "Can I trust you?"

"You know perfectly well that I would give my life for you."

The old man, pleased by the answer, let some time go by. Perhaps he was savoring the expression of loyalty; perhaps he was remembering Gottfried's theme and imagining it for strings.

"When I die, you will take it personally to my eldest son."

"Mr. Friedemann will tear it up."

"You will tell Wilhelm Friedemann," he intoned in a tired voice, interrupted by his effortful breathing, "that this theme of his brother Gottfried is the thing I love most at this moment, and that it is my wish that it be held back from the sale of my manuscripts and books."

"But how can you think that anyone would sell a manuscript..."

"You'll hear it spoken of," the master interrupted him, "but this one must not be sold."

"Why, master?"

"I don't know." As if he could see, the old man looked dreamily towards the window. "I really don't know."

"It's not music, master."

"It is music: it has come from a heart." He turned his blind face towards Kaspar's voice, putting an end to the discussion. "For now, hide it. Don't show it to my Magdalena; it would make her suffer."

He got to his feet with effort, and the boy ran to his side.

"I'm very tired. This is almost over... Do you think I'm mad, Kaspar?"

"Watch the step, master."

Kaspar helped his master, whom the effort had exhausted, to get into bed. It was early afternoon and a heavy summer shower was falling. The boy was thinking, Why aren't they back, why hasn't anybody come, please, please come, because the master had begun to call in a broken voice, Magdalena, where are you, where are my children, I'm dying, where is my music, what is this darkness... And in a hoarse, tuneless voice he sang, facing the wall,

This is enough, Lord: when you wish, release me from my bonds. Jesus, come. Oh, world, farewell. I go to the celestial mansion. I go full of certainty and peace, leaving my sorrows behind. This is enough, Lord. And Kaspar wondered if he should leave him and go for help. But he could not move from his side because his master had grasped his hand and breathed in all the air in the world. He held Kaspar's hand even harder, as if it were connecting him to life. Now he didn't breathe out. Kaspar, horrified, began to cry, because his master had just died and he was alone in the house and didn't know what to do.

The summer rain was still beating against the windows of the room. All of a sudden, Kaspar freed himself from the hand that was holding his and stood up. He'd had a frightening thought: Mistress Magdalena, Mr. Friedemann, Mr. Altnikol... everyone would blame him for the master's death because he'd allowed him to work, against instructions, and because he'd allowed him to compose music that killed him. Filled with panic, he hurried to the organ room. With tears in his eyes he found all the papers he'd written that terrible afternoon and put them in a pile. He rubbed his forehead to erase any memory of that diabolical music, as if he were capable of forgetting any note he'd heard, left the room angrily clutching the scores and headed for the stove in the kitchen. Page by page, he threw them into the fire, to erase all trace of his disobedience, all proof of his crime, until with the last sheet the dream of a madman was consumed by the fire and went smoking up the stovepipe into the gray sky of Leipzig, as if it were a life.

I REMEMBER

It happened because little Itshak was overcome by a fit of coughing. He pressed his face against his mother's body, and desperate, she drew his head to her breast, almost smothering him. But the child coughed, three irrepressible times. Though they were muffled, to the family the coughs sounded like three dreadful cannon shots. And the soldiers who were about to abandon the search heard them too.

The crackle of indiscriminate shooting immediately filled the house and the sound of breaking glass told Miriam that they'd thrown her wedding china against the window. The grandfather began to whimper to himself and Dr. Lodzer clenched his fists impotently. It took them only a moment to find the slit that opened the wall panel hiding the narrow chamber that served as the Lodzer family's hideout. They stood immobile and terrified in chiaroscuro, as if in a Rembrandt painting, lit up by the powerful Wehrmacht flashlights carried by the Ukranian SS patrol. And only the doctor could understand the hysterical shouting of the German officer, but everyone knew what it meant. And the pushing to get them out of the hiding place while Grandfather Lodzer recited the ekahs and said, The greatest among the nations has become a widow who weeps ceaselessly at night; the ways of Zion are in mourning. And to silence him the officer knocked out his three remaining teeth with a casual blow of the butt of his Mauser. Outside, on Novolipki Street, it was already dark though it wasn't yet noon, because the fog, the fear, the screams of panic, the cries of rage and the smoke of the fires were hiding the scant winter light that Adonai, God of armies, deigned to send to the ghetto. And the little ones, holding on to their mother, were saying, Where are we going, Mother?

They made them climb into a covered truck. The Lodzer family looked for the last time at the house where they'd spent the last two terrible years, and the doctor suddenly remembered all the time before the disaster, running around in his father's jewelry workshop as a child, when it wasn't a crime to cough, and the hours and hours spent studying and the days and days spent in the doctor's office on Sienna Street, the patients one after another, the births of Itshak and Edith and the great love of Miriam, now before him thinking of her beloved, powerless and defeated. She was desperately holding onto the two children, afraid that a stray gust would carry them to their death, and she felt alone, bereft, in the cutting wind. They had only the clothes on their backs, they hadn't been allowed to take even an old coat or a suitcase because the officer was so irritated (we don't have time to play hide-and-seek). Doctor Lodzer looked out of the corner of his eye at the grandfather, who was stoically enduring the pain of his damaged mouth and blaspheming silently, which was unlike him, because Elohim had abandoned him even though he was a just man. Little Itshak questioned his father with his eyes and didn't dare to say, Father, why are they doing this to us, what have we done to them? He started to cry silently because they'd been discovered on account of his cough.

The truck, in a caravan of eight or ten vehicles, disgorged dozens of terrified people onto Stawki Street, at the corner of Dzika, where a cattle train was waiting. It departed promptly, leaving the ghetto behind and passing through silent Warsaw, which was trying to look the other way, crossed the Vistula and left the city in the direction of Wolomin and Tluszcz, headed for the happy summer town of Treblinka.

They didn't strip or shave them like the others. They only locked them up with another family from their street in a room that was small, dark and very cold, with windows they hadn't even bothered to put bars on, because the jailers knew they were no longer people and had lost their survival instinct along with their dignity. And they forgot about them, as if they were so busy with the other hordes that they had no time. Or as if they didn't know what to do with them.

They spent the day in silence, their eyes wide, sitting against the wall looking towards the weak light coming in through the dirty windows. And hearing from time to time the vicious barks of the SS officers and the coarse laughter of the Ukranian volunteers. After they opened the door for the first time, to leave some crusts of moldy bread and a jar of dirty water, Doctor Lodzer reacted. He and Mr. Langfus, a jumpy old man who had lost his fabric store on Senatorskaia Street when he was interned in the ghetto, organized life in that burrow with the desperate knowledge that they had no choice but to recognize that once the thing had begun, they were inside a fateful circle, which was getting smaller day by day, and they were trying to adjust to it, giving thanks to God for his goodness, and the circle was getting even smaller until one day they wouldn't be able to praise the Lord because the circle would be as small as death. Meanwhile, though, they were surviving by thinking, by deciding that the back corner would be the latrine, that Ruth Langfus would divide the crusts into equal parts, that any adult who wasn't crying would tell stories to the children for an hour every day. But Miriam didn't participate in the desperate attempt to organize the shrinking circle where they'd been confined. She spent the days with Edith in her arms, trying to bring down her fever by looking at her or by passing her hand over her forehead, and telling stories just for her, stories that reminded her of the happy days on Ierussalimskaia Street, when she was a child who loved to hear her mother's stories. Now she had to tell them so her little girl would have a reason not to die at the age of six. Miriam thought she'd like to give her all her blood so that she would survive, so that she and Itshak would survive.

After a week, a sullen corporal entered followed by a Ukranian soldier. He swore at the stink in there and called for the Langfus family. Like silent automatons, Stanislaw Langfus and his family got organized, grandparents mixed with children, but all in line.

They left without saying goodbye, without turning their heads to look at the Lodzers one last time, so as not to infuriate the Nazi dogs. Langfus had time to hand to Miriam the wedding ring he'd been able to hide from the search to which they'd been subjected as soon as they reached Treblinka. And the Lodzers were alone, accompanied only by Itshak's little cough, which had narrowed the circle around them. And two more days of silence, wondering what had become of the Langfus family, what had become of Grandfather Stanislaw, with his blue eyes and his rolled-up sleeves, of his granddaughter Ruth, and his son-in-law and the three little ones. And everyone, except for Itshak and Edith, knew that the happy district of Treblinka had become the end of the line which they would leave only by flying up to the gray sky through the stovepipe, through the sinister tube of the chimney, as if they were a dream. They knew it but they couldn't believe it, because it was impossible that reality should be so obscene. When four days had gone by without news of the Langfuses, they understood that they would never see them again, and fell into a thick, dull silence of oblique glances, broken only by the songs that Miriam sang very sweetly to put the little girl to sleep, because she wanted her to spend the days sleeping so as not to experience that horror.

"Everybody up! Josef Lodzer!"

They'd rammed open the door, making it bang against the wall, and Edith, who'd just fallen asleep, woke up with a start but didn't even whimper because, though only six, she'd learned to keep quiet and hide her panic inside. The only thing she did was clutch her mother's hand.

"I'll be right back," the doctor said, to calm them. As he left, he looked tenderly at the grandfather, sitting in his corner, and the two children and Miriam, to take the memory of them to eternity.

"I'm sorry," said Itshak, who was still thinking about his cough.

"If you survive," the doctor whispered to them, "go to Palestine." And he disappeared, in front of the dogs.

The Hauptführer of the SS was accompanied by a thin, bald man with glasses who scrutinized Dr. Lodzer's face in order to observe his reaction to the proposal made to him.

"And what guarantee do I have that you'll keep your word?" he dared to ask.

"None. But I'm afraid you have no choice."

Accustomed to obeying, Dr. Lodzer bowed his head. In a voice of deepest sorrow, he asked:

"Who will live?"

The bald man spoke for the first time, with cultured politeness:

"That you will have to decide," he smiled sympathetically and finished the sentence, "among yourselves."

As he left, the doctor broke the rules of Treblinka by looking with hatred into the eyes of the Hauptführer and the bald man. God does not exist, he thought as they took him back to the cell.

Josef Lodzer talked with Miriam and the grandfather when the two children were sleeping. They had two hours to think about it and come to a decision. The two men allowed Miriam to cry bitterly over such impossible cruelty. When she calmed down, the grandfather insisted on reciting the ekah, as he had been doing daily since death was so close, and he recited, Remember, Jerusalem, the days of your affliction. And Miriam, her voice broken with sorrow, murmured, My soul is far from peace; now I do not know what happiness is. And Dr. Lodzer, his lips stiff, spat, My strength and my hope in Adonai have ended. He said it with such harshness that his praying of the ekah sounded like blasphemy. So that these should not be the last words of believers, the grandfather added, almost unintelligibly, Grant them, Lord, a hard heart; may that be their curse, oh, Adonai.

Itshak Lodzer felt a chill and wrapped himself in the blanket given to him by the dark-eyed girl named Hannah whose smile was like a benediction. He touched the cold barrel of the rifle and looked into the disturbing darkness. The silence of danger, fed by his own silence. All of a sudden, without warning, he had to cough. He couldn't help it. And the sound horrified him and he said, Sorry,

sorry... , like a prayer. And in a flash he saw himself in Treblinka, suffering the pain of cruelty, his fault, because it was his fault that Edith and Mother, Grandfather and Father had died. And now who knows where they were, maybe blown by the wind as far as the steppes, or deposited on the ground in a moment of calm. My dear ones, I killed you because of my cough. Even though at Raman Gat they'd taught him to forget, to erase the guilty cough from his head. The tears froze on his cheek and he pulled the blanket closer. And he saw himself with his mouth open, at the port of Haifa, holding the hand of an unknown immigrant who'd been his father, mother, sister and grandfather during the journey, and who left him at the door of the Ramat Gan Reception Center. Itshak Lodzer, twelve years old, born in Warsaw, son of Josef Lodzer and Miriam, brother of sweet Edith, grandson of Moishe Lodzer, of the Mattes family of Lodz, and therefore an eleventh-generation descendant of the great Rabbi Chaim Mattes, permanently at odds with God in spite of it all. He'd gone to Palestine in obedience to his father's last wish, along with a wave of the participants in the first aliyah bet who defied the authorities of the protectorate of Palestine and brought in those who wanted to flee in whatever way, at whatever cost, from the Europe still covered in the ashes and smoke of their brothers and sisters. For six years, in Ramat Gan, they helped him to forget, they made him vomit up the demons, and got him to sleep almost all night long, and almost stopped his pupils from fluttering and his facial muscles from twitching. They made him some very thick glasses, too thick, because his vision was aged by the horrors he'd seen. They did all that, and made him learn Hebrew and teach a few words of Yiddish to his fellow students from the Magreb, and learn Arabic and smile once in a while. But they couldn't erase the memory of that small, dark, very cold room in Treblinka.

They were years filled with frenetic activity in the adjoining school, studying violin, languages, typing, cryptography and history, so as not to leave any space in his head for remembering. When he turned seventeen, he had to give up his place in the Center to someone who needed it more. Among the options offered to him, he chose to go and work on the Ain Jarod kibbutz. When he got there he thought they would give him a hoe, but after two days of training, the first tool they gave him was a rifle to hold in one hand and three rounds of ammunition for the other. Touching the metal part of the rifle reminded him of the Luger that his poor father, Dr. Lodzer, had put into his hands after kissing him for the last time. But he didn't say anything because it seemed that at the kibbutz they trusted him with their defense. He just stood there open-mouthed with the rifle and the ammunition, and a black-haired girl came up to him with a blanket, smiling, and said, This blanket is your skin, Itshak. It'll be your only company while you're on watch. And her jet eyes were beautiful, she was named Hannah, she was in charge of supplies and was on watch that night too. And he thought it was unfair to be as ugly and shy as he was, and to have to wear thick glasses, and he didn't know how to thank her. Only after she'd moved away, handing out blankets and smiles, did he say softly, Sorry, sorry. And he looked around to see if anyone had heard. And now he'd coughed in the guard post and given away his position to possible enemies. He tried to pierce the darkness with his weak vision so as to see the flash before anyone else. Then he heard a soft, sweet swish by his ear and after it the monstrous explosion of a shot. He found himself on the ground, sitting up, and breathlessly felt his ear. A warm, sticky liquid. And he was trembling, making no sense of the cries of his companions who came rushing from the guard post. The skirmish lasted for five minutes in an infernal exchange of shots, and he didn't move, rigid, inside himself, reliving the cold dark room of Treblinka. They had to pull him, rigid, in a sitting position, from the hole he was in, and the next day they sent him back with a recommendation that he spend some time in the psychiatric hospital in Tel Aviv. They never told him how many deaths had been caused by his cough in that nighttime skirmish in Ain Jarod.

When after three years they let him live by himself again, he moved to the coastal town of Dor, fifty kilometers north of Tel

Aviv, convinced that the view of the sea, the fishermen at work and the few, small vessels going in and out of the oily port would distract him from his lacerating thoughts. The Tzahal once more considered him capable of service to a country that could allow no hands to be idle, especially if they were expert at uncovering the secrets of even the most innocent texts. His medical history and his weak vision had taken him out of the line of fire, but they shut him in a windowless room in Tel Aviv to decipher, like a cryptographer, all of the messages sent or intercepted around the world by the commandos who had just captured Eichmann in Buenos Aires. Itshak attended all the sessions of the trial in the front row, looking at the canary in his glass cage, observing him closely with his tired eyes, examining him almost without attending to the laconic answers to the tribunal's questions and letting his cough echo in his memory as many times as possible until it no longer hurt him. And he breathed easier when they executed Adolf Eichmann, as if he were the torturing Hauptführer of Treblinka. But he still didn't have the heart to visit the crypt of Yad va-Shem, because there was no therapy that could erase his fragment of Shoah from his memory, of the night when his father woke him up and whispered in his ear, You're a very brave boy, Itshak, you're a man because you're nine years old. And wide-eyed he looked at his father and behind him his mother, smiling in sorrow with Edith, no longer feverish and finally sleeping peacefully, in her arms, and Grandfather reciting another silent ekah, and being grown up made him very afraid. And his father told him, Don't worry, because we'll all live inside you. Because you're strong, you'll live and be our eyes and our memory, my son. Itshak had gone over his parents' terrible reasoning hundreds of times: to whom, oh God, to whom do we give the opportunity to escape from Hell; who must be our Orpheus? Miriam offered herself immediately in favor of anyone else, as did Josef, and they were both thinking of the children. Old Moishe held out his hands, offering to their service what little life was left to him. And then it was clear that deciding which child had to die was the most terrible of all. Miriam couldn't understand how there could be so much evil in the world; Josef, cloaked in the coolness he'd learned to cultivate as a doctor, reasoned his way from either of them, it doesn't matter, to a decision, refusing to accept that one child should be condemned by a throw of the dice, and insisting on their right to choose, and, without knowing why, he said, Itshak will live. And Miriam heard, Edith will die.

The decision was followed by a holy silence. Then Josef woke Itshak and told him that now he was a nine-year-old man. And the whole family embraced in the darkness and from that moment on Itshak had trouble sleeping at night.

During the Six Day War he was part of the reconnaissance team under the general staff on the Golan Heights. At that time he was acting as a member of the Department of Cryptography. He worked well and tried to assume the coolness affected by his father in the most difficult moments. But he couldn't pull it off, and he realized that at thirty-three (my mother's age when I killed her) he was a very weak man. He wanted to leave himself far behind, and he thought that if he moved to America or Australia, everything would be easier. After returning to Dor to put his obsessions in order by looking at the sea, the dwindling number of fishermen and the ships that passed by on the way to the port of Haifa, leaving the town in a kind of insuperable lethargy, he decided that he had to leave Israel. Twice he put his name on the emigration list, but both times his father's voice made him desist. The soft voice of his father who, once the SS had shut the door and opened the little window to observe them in safety, stood up, acting as if the whole thing were a joke, and went towards the pistol they'd left by the door. And I kept saying, Father, no, no, no, no. I won't be able to do it. And he, You have to; that's the condition for staying alive. And he pointed at the door; in Yiddish, so the people on the other side couldn't understand, he said that what the dogs wanted was for him to be a coward, because then they'd kill them all with no excuses. And I: No, Father, in that case, I'd rather die. You kill us.

And Father embraced me with all the love there could be in the world and whispered in my ear, I'll help you, my love. Neither of them thought that they were completing another terrible circle, which opened the day that Almighty God, in spite of the Alliance, ordered Abraham, so as to test him, to sacrifice his son Itshak on the hills of Moria, and which was closing in a cold, wet, dark room in the hell of Treblinka when evil decided that Itshak Lodzer was to sacrifice his father, mother, sister and grandfather, also to test him. Doctor Josef Lodzer put the pistol in his son's hand delicately, as if it were a scalpel. It was too big for him, but the doctor covered his hand with his own, as if the whole thing were a joke, and with horrifying assurance and coldness, he led Itshak to where his mother and Edith, still asleep, were lying. And Miriam sent a big kiss to her husband and to Itshak, her executioner, and she embraced Edith, who died without knowing that she was taking part in a game observed with interest on the other side of the door by two junior officers, a captain and a bald doctor. The bullet that killed Edith wounded Miriam badly, and then Dr. Lodzer didn't hesitate and made the pistol held by Itshak point at Miriam, and told her, I love you, darling, and the second shot sounded in the cold room. Grandfather lowered his head, almost touching his forehead to the ground, offering his neck with the resignation shown by the lamb offered in the ritual sacrifice, and everything in him blew up with the third shot. And Father told me, Itshak, my son, you will survive; you will live for us; you will be our eyes and our memory. Go to Palestine, put down roots, and we'll all live in Israel through you. Get married and have children and we'll all live through you. And he took Itshak's hand and put the pistol in his mouth and smiled at him as if to say, See? It's just a game. And he pulled the trigger accompanied by Itshak's dead hand, as he had done the other times. And Itshak with the Luger in his hand was incapable of thinking that now he could kill himself because at the age of nine it's impossible to think about nothingness. And the jailers came into the room smiling victoriously, and the bald doctor explained to the others that they'd just observed the defensive behavior typical of the inferior races, who were capable of the most horrible crimes in order to survive, like killing their own children and parents instead of facing the nobility of suicide. And he took the pistol that Itshak still had in his hand, ruffled the boy's hair affectionately and told him, Nothing's going to happen to you, you're going to live in the infirmary block and every once in a while you and I are going to have a little talk. And he signaled to the soldiers behind him to take him away. Itshak hardly had time to see Edith and his mother and father and grandfather for the last time. The bitter cold outside made him wake up and realize that he'd committed a terrible crime and, though they were in Treblinka because of his cough, it was his wickedness that had made him commit those murders. This idea was corroborated by the bald doctor, who had become my friend and explained to me that I was a wicked child because I'd killed my whole family to save myself, and observed my perplexed silences with infinite patience, took abundant notes in my presence and gave me candies because he was my friend. And he asked me what I was thinking and what I was dreaming. I don't know what I told him, but I never explained about the cough. And one day my friend the bald doctor disappeared without saying anything, and two hours later the Red Army came into Treblinka.

The second time he took his name off the emigration list, he realized he would never be able to leave Israel, because of the memory of the deaths he'd caused. And then, the day after his birthday, he looked for a long time at the Mediterranean, his adoptive sea, and decided that now he could visit the crypt of the memory of the camps. He chose the day when there was the least traffic, and for two hours he stared at the flame of Yad va-Shem that was the life of his family, broken by him. The name of Treblinka carved in the ground made his head hurt because of that cough, the cough that gave them away, and it was his fault. And he'd been able to carry out only one part of the pact; he'd stayed in Israel. But he had no children; he'd never married; he hadn't had the energy to make his loved ones live on in his children. And he knew that now it was too late to think about such a thing. His soul wept looking at the flame, and not once did his mind turn to the merciful Lord, because he and God hadn't talked for forty years. After he went back to Dor, good citizen Itshak Lodzer looked at the sea from his balcony, picked up the regulation army pistol and, convinced that at his age he could speculate about nothingness, lay down on the bed, waited patiently for the compassionate darkness to cover everything with its discretion, and put the gun in his mouth, as he remembered his father doing. But he didn't smile, because he had no son to deceive. If he was incapable of honoring the whole pact, at least he could join them. Maybe because the metal was cold or because he was afraid of his own act, a cough betrayed him, he had an irresistible attack of coughing. But now he didn't have the body of his mother to press against so Hell wouldn't hear him. Some strange scruple made him wait until the coughing stopped and the silence of great moments was restored. And he fired, forty years after the first cough, with the hope that sorrow could no longer hurt him.

FINIS CORONAT OPUS

*H*orresco referens, *said Saint John before the Seventh Seal, and I say the same, friends, now that, after a period of intense training, I am at home in the Truth, the Here and Now, the best site, the right place at the right time, surrounded by bird shit and stink, which the Lord has provided expressly for me, the Returnee. The Lord has given me shelter and put me right up front, with a generous no-man's-land and lots of noisy traffic between me and them. And a nice breeze to make up for how sticky and hot it's been.*

I'm going to go back, friends, only a few weeks. The whole thing started when Miqui told me it was a piece of cake. That's what he told me: a piece of cake, Quiquín. If I'd known then how I was going to suffer, I would've gone looking for Miqui at his Israeli beach house in Salou and hauled him by the balls into the Here and Now, so he could see what I'm going through. He'd shit in his pants because he's a person who's scared to death of death. So the whole thing began when I spent an entire afternoon and evening building myself up, as patiently as that masochist Job. And pumping yourself up is a bad idea. A hell of a bad idea. Inside you're reciting the prayer that says, I'll show you guys how to make plans, you assholes. But the damage is done. And it's so bad you have no other choice.

It's easy to pick up girls, that jerk Miqui told me. So I thought, okay, and I went into the Cafè de la Mirada looking around, ready to party, I mean with good intentions, to get some, you know. The first one I saw was pudgy, with a very short skirt, and she really knew how to handle that tray full of stuff, and amazingly she knew how to keep from tripping on the steps, because the place is all up and down.

I sniff Crimson, Lord, and that's the greatest pleasure that Life in the Here and Now can bring. I sniff Crimson through my blessed Hearing and everybody, thanks to the Walkman, is absent lovers and everybody is Kerouac and Cassidy driving around in Paris. Life is beautiful and so I want to tip my hat to Fate: the girl is right for me. Come on, Quiquín, don't screw up, get off to a good start; keep your hand steady; perfect, she's mine, she's mine. Bingo. BINGO, Quiquín. She's perfect. I'm in the right place. Miqui, Mom, if you could only see me.

I did trip, on the first stair, because there's no light in the place, which I think they do to save money. She walked past me saying to herself, three Cokes, a SevenUp, two drafts, as if it were a litany, three stuffed olives, ora pro nobis, an order of anchovies, ora pro nobis, turris eburnea, four beers. She didn't even look at me. I didn't like that. That pushes my buttons, but I was being patient, see. I didn't even do anything, I just damned Miqui to hell. That's all I did then. But it really gets to me when they act like I'm not even there.

I sat down at the first empty table I saw and I was already pissed off because the illegal immigrant in charge of ambience had put on shitty *Heroin* like this was the Factory and those assholes were inviting everybody to Direct Intravenous Perdition. Hearing Velvet makes me want to throw up. It was a bad beginning, friends, way too seventies. It was time to get out of there. But I stayed. That's why the whole thing started, because I stayed. With Velvet boring into my ears. Why the hell did I have to go through all that if all I wanted was to pick up a girl? And on top of everything else, the so-called music was too loud. I hate it loud because then you have to pay attention to the music and you can't get into the pickup thing. If it were up to me, I'd burn down all the discos with the Communists, teenagers, street people, disc jockeys and Bosnians inside. All of them. If I have to spend so many hours there, they should turn down the volume, right? Or turn it off, for God's sake, before I lose it because I have sensitive ears and all those decibels just drill their way into my brain as if I'd spent the whole day on a cell phone. That's why I'm so sensitive to background music and I turn right around and get off the elevator if it's playing Mozart and I refuse to get on planes. Well, I've only been on a plane in the Return to the Promised Land episode. And when they'd had enough of the Velvet Underground, because it was going on and on, he goes for contrast and puts on *Finlandia* by Sibelius, which is even more retro. Like we were in the metro, and this was the perfect time and place to listen to that drivel. I felt like killing the person in charge of ambience, of choosing the music, right there. If there is somebody responsible, because sometimes things just happen, for no reason, just because. Thinking about that just wears me out. It irritates me, it wounds my sensibility that they don't know that what gives a place style, especially if it's new, like the Café de la Mirada, is something like King Crimson. And people weren't even paying attention, as if they couldn't even hear the music. People are really something, you play the soundtrack of their lives and nothing, they don't give a shit. For a minute I felt like killing all of them. But then I got myself under control. I'd only been in the place for four minutes and thirteen seconds and things were going downhill fast. It was very hard to control myself because the place was full of old people, Bosnians, hippies, Norwegians and homeless, nobody normal like me. That's when she appeared. Slender, wearing just enough eye makeup— you have to describe everything—blondish, with a smile on her lips and gum between her teeth lighting up her mouth, which I would have planted a kiss on then and there, but I just held on, like Saint George before the Dragon of Temptation... because when I'm good I'm very, very good. She still didn't know that I was beginning to pump myself up. The girl, with a tray in one hand and a cloth in the other, goes and leans over and lets me see her promising cleavage, and then I thought, Hey, Miqui, you're right, it is fucking easy, and

I picked up on her smile and said, What's up, and she winked at me and said, What'll you have, sir?

Listen, in a place like this, with waitresses who're, you know, friendly, it's insulting when they call you Sir. That girl was saying You're thirty-seven, you idiot, don't you even notice you're going bald, you fool, you've broken up with three different women and everybody knows about it, you haven't even been able to finish a lousy university degree, what are you doing here? You think you're Tarzan? But I controlled myself, pumping myself up even more, and I said, Don't call me Sir, sweetie, like that, politely. And then they go and put on *Child in Time*, a mess with no sense of rhythm and stupid crappy lyrics, and I was starting to get pissed off, pumping myself up, with Gillan's high little neuter voice, he's worse than Farinelli. I'd take all the queers and all the Bosnians and I'd boil them in a pressure cooker. Quousque tandem abutere, Deep Purple, patientia nostra? says Saint Matthew 13:22, which I repeat and make mine. I mean, I don't think you always have to score the first time...

If I weren't sniffing Crimson and traveling with Neal and Jack through the streets of Paris, I wouldn't be able to take any more, it seems like even from the Here and Now I'd be able to hear how this guy gives orders. I think she's looked in the direction of Here and Now and I can't have that because I'm God, I kill when I want and I don't have to explain anything to anybody. Besides, from this distance the guy looks like Pepus. I'd like to get a look at his neck, but it's as short as the sleeves on a vest. Just a minute, Pepus, the guitars have gone back to that impossible rhythm, oh, oh, hearing the Truth in the Truth. Saint Robert Fripp, ora pro nobis... Where were we? Pepus. That fucking son of a bitch Pepus. It's your turn, man. Can you imagine being Pepus? There. Calm down Let's see... Bingo. Right in his nonexistent neck. You're something else, Quiquín.

...but if a girl turns up her nose I tell her, No problem, I've got a full schedule and I wouldn't have had five minutes for you anyway. And that's when they soften up and when you say, Now get screwed and I'm gonna find somebody else. And she just keeps looking at me, moving her gum around with a shit-eating grin, and she comes back with, What'll you have, sir, as if I hadn't said, Don't call me Sir, honey. I decided to be nice and pump myself up even more, if that were virtually possible.

"A nice cold Estrella and the time you get off work, Jane," I said with a smile.

That's what I'm like: if somebody wants a fight, I bow down and bend like bamboo because, you ignoramuses, it takes two to fight, as Lao Tse teaches. And I looked back at her with the same shit-eating grin.

Now it looks like they're starting to realize that something's going on. People are really slow. It's like they walk around without looking at one another, ignoring one another as He has ignored everybody.

At that moment Our Father Time had had enough of Gillan's yelps and we were supposed to listen to Barber's *Adagio for Strings*, the most saccharine thing ever to emerge from the human mind, and I kept on holding back and grinning shittily like the waitress. I was starting to notice how hot it was that time of year, which was made worse by the vulgarity of the DJ, the hired gun of the Bad Taste Mafia.

"We don't have Estrella. It'll have to be Voll Damm."

"What the hell do you mean you don't have Estrella?" It just came out; I know I shouldn't have said it, but what's done is done. And Samuel Barber kept on greasing up the walls and nobody even noticed. Maybe that's the worst thing: that people don't notice whether it's Lou Reed or a fucking Bosnian tone poem, for God's sake.

"I mean we're out. So it's Voll Damm or come back tomorrow, sir."

So she was still calling me Sir and she was inviting me to get lost. And chewing gum the whole time. So instead of blowing up I thought of Luke 2:27 where he says Be more whorish than the Guineans and more clever than the whores, and I didn't react. I said Fine, honey, a Voll Damm. And when do you get off?

"Go to hell."

See, friends? She stopped calling me Sir. She didn't give me time to say, And what time is Go to Hell, exactly? Ten? Eleven? Eleven twenty-three? Huh? She'd walked away, nose in the air, to get the beer, and I'm thinking so hard that, if it weren't for the saccharine Barber, you could probably hear my brain whirring from outside my cranium. Three columns away, I saw the fatty laughing like crazy by a table where two boys were being very nice to her. The little pig probably wanted to make it with both of them and I jotted this down in my memory book. The Barber wasn't over yet and all of a sudden Jane was right there. She banged the bottle and the mug down on the table.

"Four euros."

She tossed the tab as if it were confetti, and it fell into the puddle made by the sweating bottle. Four euros for a beer, hell, even if it's a fashionable bar, come on, even if it did just open, four euros for a beer isn't right. I felt like I could hear the gum rubbing against Jane's very white teeth.

"Do I have to pay now?"

I said that because I'd just realized that I didn't have enough fuel in my coin purse. And what did she do? She didn't say yes or no. She just stood there waiting. Then I noticed her breasts. Amazing, I admit. I closed my wallet and said, How much did you say it was, love?

Jane snorted, looked around as if she were searching for a friendlier client to do business with, and stared impatiently at me. Her voice was shaking with an anger I didn't deserve.

"Four thirty-five," the little whore said, smiling like a bishop's secretary.

"You told me four euros!" I yelled, shocked.

"So why did you ask me?"

A logical woman. I took a gulp of Voll Damm to try and repair my ego, which was a little damaged. Then I saw the damp tab and you know what it said, friends? Two eighty-five. Two euros and eighty-five cents, it said. It's infuriating, so infuriating that I can't think about it because it makes my heart pound.

"Here it says two eighty-five!" I said this objectively, sure that I was on the side of the angels. And so, buttressed by my strict sense of justice as a son of Hammurabi and Charles Lynch, I opened my wallet again, reached inside and left two puny euros on the table, to get back at her.

"Go fuck yourself," I said just as, finally, Barber was becoming history and some ancient nonexpert was trying to refresh our neurons with Jethro Tull. Jane—not because of Tull, because she was part of the immense majority who live without listening—froze her tongue, her lips, her teeth and her gum. After a few seconds she blew a pretty little dry bubble and popped it.

"Do you want me to call Pepus?"

I've never known anybody named Pepus. Well, now I do. But before meeting Jane, I didn't know anybody named Pepus. But it didn't seem right that she would say, Do you want me to call Pepus, as if everybody on earth knew who Pepus was. Back when I was in college, the way things worked was that if a woman who just popped her gum asked, Do you want me to call Pepus, you knew Pepus was a refrigerator with fists like hammers and a very short neck, fuse and hair. So, I decided to retreat, but I immediately wrote down the incident in my memory book and thought about the first letter to the Corinthians 5:2, when the Apostle to the Gentiles says that the Bosnians should be delivered to Satan for the perdition of their flesh. I took my wallet out of my pocket and left the biggest bill I had on the wettest part of the table.

"For your services," I blessed her.

Jane took the bill and disappeared without responding to my provocation, which shows that she really was as slutty as they come.

Let's see, let's see, the guy with the white hair who looks all worried and wants to run everything... Don't mess with me, because I... Oh... for the fourth and last time the guitars according to Saint Fripp, the most godly crim of all, the eternal crim, the essence, the DNA of Crimson, I said not to look over here. I don't know why they don't realize they're all in danger. My God, when people can't comprehend the movement of God they become animals in God's eyes, they're like beetles, or ants, poor things. Take a deep breath. Goodbye, man with white hair. And that's three, Quiquín. Now it looks like everybody's getting really nervous. It took them long enough.

Jethro Tull. Okay. You can smell the mothballs, but okay. The people at the next table, you could put on ballads and they'd keep right on talking without trashing the place. You can't believe how out of it people are. They spend the whole day talking so they won't have to think and then at the end of the day they're exhausted, a little pill just in case, and that way they don't have to open their memory books and worry about indigestion.

Jane brought my change very correctly, on a little plate. She set it so carefully on the table that I, drinking beer and helping Jethro redeem humanity, raised my eyes, totally surprised.

"Five minutes after eleven," she said.

"Excuse me?" I'd moved on to a different war.

"I get off at five after eleven." She pointed, I suppose in the direction of the kitchen. "At the door that opens onto the street out back, okay?"

Friends, I was amazed. So that tight-ass stuff was an act: she seemed like she was all uninterested in front of everybody else and what she really wanted was to get into a relationship that involved an exchange of bodily fluids. I remember thinking, Miqui, you're a great guy. I looked at my watch: I only had half an hour to wait until five after eleven.

"I'll be there, Jane," I said gallantly. For a minute, only a minute, I drifted away, and when I came back they were playing, believe it or not, the Pixies. As if the no-taste idiot in charge of the music wanted to share my happiness. If man is five and the Devil is six, God is seven, repeated the Pixies. Where's my wallet, to put away the change. The Pixies, Barber, the Underground, Sibelius, Jethro Tull... If that's musical taste, may God come down and damn the person in charge.

The street out back wasn't a street but a dirty, narrow alley. It was well lighted, though. I tried every door I went past to see if it was open, because I didn't have the faintest idea which one belonged to the place. Finally I recognized the logo of the Cafè de la Mirada on a door painted green. That was it. I leaned against the wall, satisfied, thinking about Jane's gum, which was the first thing I'd ask for. I looked up, towards the stars, towards some friendly constellation. But the streetlight above me was blocking my imagination. Then I heard the whistle.

No, not true. I didn't hear the whistle then. She was one of those pigs who make people wait. Eleven. I'd gotten there at a quarter to, of course, but eleven came and five after and then seven after and she didn't show up. And when the bells rang for eight minutes after, still nothing. Then I got pissed off; I've explained that I'm a guy with a full schedule and I won't be kept waiting. At a quarter after—a quarter after!—I heard a kind of whistle, as if somebody were calling me.

Now they're figuring out what's going on. You just have to make up your mind calmly. Take this, old lady. And you, for being Bosnian. And you, for being a Communist. No, don't go there. Quiquín, don't get overwhelmed. Come on, man!... Communists have always been the hardest nuts to crack, said Saint Paul in his second to Timothy 3:12. Because Crimson was on for the fourth time in a row and I, friends, didn't want to go crazy obsessive about music that would make holes in my memory and keep me from thinking about others, I put the FR50 down on the floor very carefully, took out the Apostle Fripp tape, kissed it and threw it into the void, immolated for the good of Humanity. I wished that Crimson would make its way into the head of a cop and be recorded in his repressive brain. Now, friends, I put the Holy Tape into the machine, the Musical Discovery of the Century, the Second Part of The Last Recital of Pere Bros, the Find from the little store on the Osterhausgate, the unknown, lawful, real, stimulating, imaginative, living, supermodern, ultraclassic Contrapunctum of Fischer, a musical story for minds that are lucid, awake and imaginative like mine. And, when I heard the opening theme, the tears in my eyes almost, almost made me stop wanting to do justice. That son of a bitch Pere Bros could really play. He was so good that I, Quiquín of Barcelona, understood and accepted the degree of desperation that drove him to commit suicide after having helped to create such beauty.

I thought there was only one way in but apparently not, because I saw the front of a 4x4 coming around the corner and stopping in front of me. Motorized Jane. And she called me from inside the car. I was under the streetlight, where she could see me perfectly, and I tapped three or four times on my watch, offended, or maybe five or six, or seven or eight or nine times. And only then, when I'd defended my honor, did I get in the 4x4 thinking about the gum, thinking that I felt like chewing that gum and then... But I didn't have a chance to say what I hadn't even finished thinking I'd do with Jane after asking for her gum, because she interrupted me.

"Come on, get in," she said. And, like in a miracle, just from hearing her voice I saw her breasts and I thought that life was good. I hadn't thought that for twelve years. Twelve years and five months. Maybe because I was thinking that it had been one hundred fifty-nine months since I'd broken up with Lidia, eighty-six since I'd broken it off with that whore Mercedes, and eight hundred twenty-two days since I ran away from Sonia and the world opened before me up north, like in a movie, I didn't notice that in the 4x4 there was no gum and no Jane, but rather a refrigerator with short hair, no neck and, if I had to judge from the way he was drumming his thumbs on the steering wheel, very little patience. Ars longa, vita brevis, said Saint James in his epistle. And I really was about to have a short life, because Pepus grabbed me by the shirt and banged me up against the rough wall of the alley, all without getting out of the car. So imagine, friends, what was going to happen when he got out of the 4x4: he picked me up off the ground by the hair and held me up to his stinking breath. He worked things out with his fists; he broke three of my teeth, bruised my spleen and cracked three ribs. I was interested in turning that monologue into a dialogue more productive for both participants, but I have to confess that I was unable to respond properly because I was thinking about my long, fruitful and surprising life, especially after leaving the seminary to the great delight of my mother and, I suppose, my father and starting to handle women with kid gloves for fear of getting burned and having decided that the words of the apostle Robert Fripp, nosce te impsum, would have to be the guiding light of my life from then on, After beating on me for a long time the maniac must have been worn out because he ended it with one last roundhouse punch. I saw that nice light show and the world inside me disappeared.

From what I've deduced after a week of convalescence, Pepus put me in the 4x4 and took me out of the car some distance from the Cafè. I don't know how, but I don't think he was too gentle because my clothes were all covered with mud and weeds. And so I woke up in the morning on the Vallvidrera highway with a terrible headache, with pain when I breathed, blood in my mouth, my teeth altered for the worse and, in general, an impressive resemblance to Saint Lazarus. I felt like Job and I didn't like the role, so I decided to go back home. It took me three hours to get there, an enriching Crossing of the Desert, an illuminating Road to Damascus, a fruitful Mystic Revelation. Animam pro anima, oculum proóculo, dentem pro dente, says Our Lord Jesus Christ, and I made this evangelical maxim mine and when my soul and my body were restored, I went to steal the boar rifle that Papa had hung on the wall in Sardinia, in an area where no one has ever seen a boar unless it's braised with scallions or stewed with chocolate. I say steal because once I was there I remembered that Papa had sold the house six or seven years ago. Regrets aside, I decided that I couldn't let the trip go to waste and also, the guy hadn't changed the lock on the door and, on top of that, his rifle, a real Swedish FR50, had a telescopic sight, so if anybody was to blame, it would be his grievous negligence. And the new owner was hiding the box of ammunition in the same place where Papa had hidden it. So I loaded the rifle with his bullets and myself with patience, searching, searching without haste, thinking God will provide, thinking that in the Gospel according to Fripp the Lord says, Do you not see the birds, how they fly and fornicate untroubled, dammit? In this way God protects and watches over all his creatures; how, then, can you think he will not protect you, Quiquín of Barcelona, you who are his favorite? Inflamed by this faith, I searched, inquired, and finally found the perfect site, the right place to do what I had to do, between the top floor and the roof of the ideal building, in the stratum called No Man's Land. Wow, the third or fourth variation, an imitatio in four voices, what a wealth of ideas. Why was Fischer unknown until now, God? Why did the Holy Fisherman hide from us the essence of his art?

A whole day inside this dovecote full of bird shit and dead pigeons and a filthy, absurd stink, with an additional problem, which is that I have to bend over all the time and sometimes I stand up without thinking and smack myself on the back of the head, which I think is bleeding. But the thing is that the magical and camouflaged opening to the Holy Dovecote is directly across from my target. It's the Lord's will and for that reason I've baptized this Sacred Dovecote with the name of Truth, though some call it Here and Now. Another defect of the Sacred Dovecote is that it's fucking hot inside. But if to find this perfect hiding place it was Lord's Will that first I had to neutralize the doorman of the building, who rudely and insultingly insisted on knowing where I was going with that shotgun, the fact that the find has had to overcome these obstacles makes it even more valuable in the eyes of God, in the eyes of Humanity, in the eyes of History. I can hardly move and every once in a while my legs cramp, but I praise the Lord for showing me the Site and for being able to ignore the inconvenience first with absent lovers, absent lovers, absent lovers, a cassette tape with nothing on it but Neal, Jack, Me, and now the seventh and last variation of Fischer the Saint, which will be with me until God says Enough... Hey, look, finally, shit! I chose right! God finally said Enough; what I've been waiting for for eighteen minutes and twenty-nine seconds: after so much trouble, finally, nosy Jane has stuck her head out, all jittery. She just couldn't wait. I'm not going to give her a second chance. Okay, be still, honey. Done. I just hung a well-deserved red medal over her heart. I hope her gum won't end up in the wrong place, poor thing. Honesta mors turpi vita potior. Amen.

I'm going to try and include everybody in the cast, oh Barcelona friends, especially Bosnians, the homeless, Norwegians, old people and Communists. I'll be here as long as I can stand it and the sweat doesn't make me close my eyes. And I'll set aside the last bullet, to erase my memory book Here and Now. I already said it a minute ago when I began this Second Epistle: horresco referens.

BALLAD

Zorka stopped smiling when they took away the only thing she loved, her son, a hulking boy in his twenties who still drooled and who hadn't been able to learn to read because of the twisted connection between his eyes and his head. But he was good enough to go to war and they took him.

Zorka often thought about her Vlada and she would cry bitterly when she imagined a thousand bullets piercing his empty head, or godless and soulless soldiers making fun of him because he was always smiling and showing the unpleasant hole in his mouth. Zorka got into the habit of sitting in the dining room, the cloth with the crowded flowers spread over the table, her hands on top of it, her gaze fixed on some spot of light, letting the hours go by remembering her son's idiot giggle. One afternoon her memory got away from her and she thought about Vlada's infancy, before anyone could say that he was a little short on words and ideas, and she still hoped to bring up a normal child. And her thoughts went even farther back, to the first days she'd lived alone, because a runaway horse had killed Petar, the admirable Petar Stokovic, the strongest man in the village, and life had left her pregnant with Vlada and open-mouthed in astonishment. And she remembered the time when, still a maiden, she was the pretty girl from the Black House and her dour brothers managed the property as best they could and she asked nothing else of life. Zorka of the Black House remembered these happy things to forget, for at least a few instants, her sorrow over Vlada's laugh, which grew sillier and sillier as time went by. And in this way Zorka's days seemed shorter.

As time went by and her thoughts were so much in the past, she forgot to talk with people and started living on wine and salt cod so as not to have to cook, not to have to do anything, to have more time to meditate on the son taken away by godless and fatherless soldiers. Every day, she would go out in the middle of the afternoon, raising dust by dragging her tired feet beyond the last houses to contemplate the road down which they'd taken him. And she would stay there until the end of the day, when the shadows grew long and people started saying, There's Zorka, it's time to start thinking about supper. And the neighbor women didn't dare make conversation because her glance had grown so sour.

The Black House had always been a silent place, as if the walls could foresee and remember the death that would shortly befall them. That's why the neighbor women failed to hear Zorka whimpering at the table, and they wondered more than once what that poor woman was doing shut up like that, and crossed themselves thinking how she could take the blows of life like a stone, feeding on the bitterness of her tears. And Zorka spent hours motionless at the table until the day when exactly three months had gone by since they took her son, and she wanted to cry very hard, to give vent to the rage that had built up in her for ninety days. And so her neighbors couldn't hear, she put her head in the oven and howled half the night until she collapsed.

When people started to say that the gunfire was getting closer and started to see rotting bodies floating down the Rzav, Zorka tried to draw strength from her desolation, and right at noon she would go to the Ice Bridge and sit on a stone by the bank to watch the hours and the dead go by in the river that, when she was little, had produced carp and pleasure. At first she watched anxiously, in case she might recognize her son, but what she did was imagine the dark death in the eyes of the drowned and she waved goodbye to them and said, Goodbye, my children, why have you killed one another when just moments ago you were playing hide-and-seek, and they didn't answer her, though some of them looked at her with fear still on their faces. And now, standing at their doors, people said, Look, Zorka's going to the river, poor woman, it's already time for dinner. And they said, May Almighty God have mercy on her, and they went inside, because since the Rzav had started to carry bodies there was a curfew in the village after noon.

One day, Zorka ran into a gang of soldiers who were heavily armed but dirty and ragged, unshaven from days in the forest, and looking for trouble. They told her rudely that she couldn't be out at that hour, or any hour, that they were in charge. And because she looked at them vacantly and said nothing, the corporal warned her that nobody messed with him, and he had orders to shoot anything that moved, including cats and dogs. She paid them no mind and went on towards the river, because it was noon and she had to go see her dead pass by. The corporal called to her again and his shouts echoed off the walls of the houses and pierced the ears of the terrified neighbors. Zorka, as if listening to the wind blow, kept on, dragging her feet and raising dust. The corporal swore and barked out the order to fire; the godless and soulless soldiers hesitated as they watched her walk away, and one of them thought, This isn't right, it isn't right, she's just a crazy old lady. The corporal repeated the order, his voice hoarse with rage. Then one of the soldiers put his rifle to his shoulder, a magnificent FR50 that before the war some lucky man had used to hunt boar, fixed the woman's back in the telescopic sight, and fired. Zorka of the Black House fell like an abandoned sack of clothes. The soldier went up to her, pleased with his marksmanship, looked at her amazed, raised his head and shouted.

"Look. I hit her and she's still moving."

Zorka, badly wounded, turned her face to the sky, to let her soul escape more easily, and breathed wearily. She felt no pain because she'd cried all her tears long ago. Then she looked at the soldier's face, widened her eyes and extended her hand. The words she said were understood only by the stones because they were accompanied by a bubble of blood made thick and dark by suffering. And she thought, Poor child, he's lost another tooth, they're not taking care of him. The soldier was amused by the dark bubble, and, still laughing, he put the barrel of the rifle to Zorka's forehead. She was shuddering desperately, not from fear but from the desire to make herself understood in spite of the bubble of blood. The shot burst her skull and the soldier howled, triumphant, happy,

"She finally stopped moving! Finally!"

And with his sleeve he wiped the drool that trailed from his mouth and went, fatherless, soulless and stupidly smiling, to where the gang was.

POCI

I (2)

There were ten people on the elevator and he wasn't the only one carrying flowers. On the second floor some kind of security guard got on after winking at a very pretty nurse. The three people with bouquets got off on the fourth floor. As if he knew the clinic by heart, he headed down the corridor towards room 439. A woman wearing a coif and carrying a tray full of things he couldn't identify came out of the room next door. When he got to the door he was looking for, he paused for a few seconds, wiped away the sweat that beaded his upper lip whenever he was nervous, breathed out hard, and knocked discreetly three times. The voice saying "Come in" was muffled, with a note of curiosity. It seemed to him there was also a little hopefulness in that "Come in." He went in, a little formal, holding out the roses as if they were a calling card. All of a sudden he saw her there, sitting on a sofa in the ancient posture of delighted exhaustion typical of new mothers. She had obviously just nursed the baby, who was now lying in the crib. He closed the door without making a sound and turned to the woman, who hadn't moved from the sofa and was looking right at him, noticing the sweat that shone on his upper lip. Now her voice sounded cracked: "Who are you?"

The man, with a polite smile, leaned over the woman to offer her the flowers. And instinctively she took them and moved as if to smell them. That's why she didn't see the black eye of the silencer on the pistol that appeared among the roses. The bullet went in through her open mouth; there was nothing to hear but a gentle, almost sweet poc! The woman leaned back softly on the sofa, as if her exhaustion were infinite, as well as ancient. Not a whimper. Two delicately dropped the flowers onto the woman's lap. Then he looked towards the crib, shook his head, wiped the sweat off his lip with the hand holding the pistol and looked at the newborn, who was trying out his thumb. Delicately, almost lovingly, he brought the barrel up against the base of its skull. The pistol went poc!.

It wasn't until he got to the airport in Le Bourget and had smoked half a pack of Gitanes that he managed to get his heart to start working normally. And that was just the beginning.

ll (1)

One had spent the flight from Paris looking straight ahead, as if genuinely interested in the folding tray on the back of the seat ahead of him. And he didn't look even once at the scenery out the window. He refused the dinner and the drink without looking the stewardess in the eye, as if he didn't want to lose his focus for even a moment. As if he wanted to do everything in his power to be in the right place at the right time with the cigarette and the whisky after work. He looked only twice at the reddish head of the man he'd been told to eliminate. Okay to kill. He was called Zero and he was very easy to follow because of the bright color of his hair. Now that he was looking at him for the second time, on the other side of the aisle, a few seats ahead, he realized that Zero wasn't hiding the briefcase attached to his wrist by a kind of sturdy-looking handcuff. He was reading *France Soir* and didn't feel One's glance pass over the back of his neck.

Five seats back, Two was watching One look at something ahead of him. He'd found it odd that Three had ordered him to follow One and wait; he could have finished him off in the bathroom in the airport, once his heart had started to beat normally. He leaned back; he followed orders and he'd do One in Barcelona just like they'd told him to. It was easier to obey, not ask questions, and bide his time. Natalie would be happy; as soon as he finished work he'd go back to Paris and invite her out for a great dinner. The most irritating thing was having to spend hours on planes that didn't allow smoking. He considered it insulting but was going to have to get used to it. In fact, he was already used to working like this, always being a Two in pursuit of a One. He was One once; he'd felt bad about it, really. Well, the way he felt about what happened at the clinic. But, work is work. Anyway, the thing that he... What?

"Would you like more coffee, or a soft drink, or...?"

"A whisky."

The stewardess blocked his view of One and for a few seconds he panicked. But he smiled and forced himself to relax: how could he escape? Besides, according to the complicated rules of Three's game, One had no idea who Two was. Hey, he didn't know that Two existed any more than human beings are aware of death like a worm inside them.

"Two is the death of One," he said, imprudently, out loud.

"Excuse me?" The stewardess was handing him the glass of whisky.

"No, no, I was..." And he made a vague gesture that meant it didn't matter. The stewardess continued on her way, and Two could see that One was still looking ahead of him, as if at another passenger.

Zero, who didn't know that's what he was called, made a vague gesture to refuse the coffee, or soft drink, or... Although the handcuff that attached him to the briefcase bothered him a little, he was absolutely faithful to the procedure he'd followed on the eighty-two previous trips. He was pretending to be a perfumier carrying formulas and samples from one branch to another so that, if he had to, he could justify taking the briefcase with him everywhere. In fact, it contained, aside from four innocent papers designed to distract any customs officials who might be curious about the contents, the notebook he'd just stolen from Three, showing the bank statements for the past five years that he'd done collection for the business, and condemning Three and all of his family to death. Because even just the first five pages of that bankbook were enough to paper him over for life.

Of course Zero was afraid. Very afraid. Because his hours were numbered: make the payment, turn the book over to the police in Barcelona, with the delayed-access system to cover his tracks, call the clinic to tell her to do what she had to do, and meet her after the eight-hour flight to Rio. Meet them. Because the three that's a crowd was what had made them, him and the woman, decide that Zero had to change his life. His wife didn't know that Zero was called Zero, of course. Or that she was called Double Zero and their son Little Zero. We are always ignorant of the plans of the gods. Very afraid, was Zero: but things had to turn out according to their very careful plans. He'd turned down what the stewardess offered because the pressure of the situation had upset his stomach.

III (o)

In the hotel dining room, Two fell in love with a table for one next to the window. He found it very strange that One, who didn't have to stay in that hotel, should be eating supper there. That's his problem, he thought. He just had to follow orders. It was irritating, but he settled down to sharing a dining room with his victim and lit a cigarette so he could hide behind the smoke. Maybe it was to avoid unpleasant thoughts that he imprudently ordered an 1864 from the maitre d' and a very rare steak to go with it. The maitre d' raised his eyebrows because it had been two years since he'd ordered a whole bottle. No doubt because One noticed the bottle ordered by the man sitting by the window, he ordered one too, and the maitre d', happy as a clam, said to the headwaiter that life is full of surprises. Yes, it certainly is. Especially if Three has planned them that way.

While One was tasting the wine—magnificent, well preserved, well aged—he saw something he didn't like at all. Zero was coming into the dining room with an unknown woman. That wasn't in the program. Zero was supposed to have supper in the hotel and then go right to bed, because the money contact was scheduled for early the next morning. But he was such a smart guy that... Oh, and the way they moved and talked, it looked like it wasn't the first time they'd seen one another. So Zero had a lover in Barcelona. Or maybe she was... One had understood that Zero had a wife in Paris. She probably saw her lover every time Zero was away making contacts. He noticed that he was still carrying the briefcase, even now.

"How about that table?" Zero gestured with his free hand.

"Perfect." The woman walked over to it, politely acknowledged a man at the next table who was working away at a big steak, and waited for Zero to pull out her chair. One, who'd observed every detail, concluded that she was a working girl. The couple sat down, the waiter moved into position with the menus, and before they started to look at them, she pointed to the handcuff and the briefcase that was supposed to kill him.

"What's that? An engagement bracelet?"

"No." He looked around, his glance passing over One and Two, and signalled to the maitre d' as he turned to the woman. "Shall we go ahead and order wine, Mary?"

"Katty."

When the maitre d' came over, Zero smiled at him. "Bring us some red wine. The best one you've got."

"An 1864, for example?"

The maitre d', when Zero couldn't see him, winked at the woman and moved away shaking his head: he couldn't believe it. The woman kept at him.

"Why are you carrying it like that, attached?"

"Secret formulas."

"Wow. So you're a spy?"

"No, the opposite: I don't want to be spied on." To make her shut up, "Perfume."

"And we're supposed to go to bed with that?"

Zero laughed. He liked the joke. This was the first time he was doing things a different way. Usually he waited to screw until the job was done, but because this time he had to hurry off, he wanted to do things backwards. For supper, they had a good wine and a little something to eat.

IV (2)

At the hour when dogs take their owners out for a walk, One went back to his hotel, after making sure that Zero had gone to his room to perform an uncomfortable ménage à trois with the woman and the briefcase, and Two resisted the temptation to follow him and went up to his room. In the hall on the tenth floor, the maid for that floor, her cart full of those little details that make it a pleasure to stay at our hotel, gave him a professional smile highlighted by an anachronistic gold tooth, and went on her way. Two let his mind wander for half an hour, looking out the window at the lights and more lights from the nighttime traffic on the Rambla de Catalunya and thinking that being a hit man wasn't so bad if they paid you this much and you had to perform just a few times a year. And he was always covered, especially if he worked for the enigmatic Three, who had things taken care of before they even happened. He didn't recognize One as the man with the moustache who was slouching along in front of the movie theater. It was too far to be able to make him out. Nor did One, who was now heading back to his hotel, look up to see if Two was looking at him, because he didn't know he existed, any more than Three knew he was called Three, because if he knew that, then he might have guessed at the presence of Two, who was now a shadow in the window that looked at him without seeing. Another thing Two didn't know was that there, in his own hotel, Zero, who hadn't been informed that he was now a widower and the father of a dead child, was hard at it with a woman and a briefcase, and that Zero was nothing more than his victim's victim and so a victim of himself, just as my friends' friends are friends of mine.

V (1)

The payment was made in the chosen place, the lookout on Tibidabo. One watched as Zero, still attached to the briefcase, opened it with the secret combination, put the packet handed to him by an unknown man inside and headed for the phone booth conveniently hidden by bushes, paying no attention to the early-morning panorama of Barcelona swarming below him. One had to wait for Zero to make the call, also unexpected, before going after him.

"No, connect me with room 439!" yelled Zero, irritated by the ineptitude of the operator at the clinic.

"Who's calling, please?"

"What?"

"Who's calling?"

He hesitated for a moment and then gave his name and added that he was the husband of his son's mother. He thought it was odd that the operator covered the receiver and said something unintelligible to somebody. And then, as if she were following instructions:

"Where are you calling from, sir?"

"Why do you care?"

The hesitation that followed gave him a very bad feeling. The operator, in a poker voice: "Please hold. The Director is going to take your call."

He didn't hang up because it was impossible for them to trace the call in Paris. But he could smell that something was rotten. He couldn't smell that, behind him, One was opening the door of the phone booth, bringing the silencer up to his ear, and poc! making the family complete and forcing his resignation with characteristic professionalism. From the dangling receiver One could hear the cries of the Director, who was saying *Allô, allô, monsieur?*, unaware that monsieur was now ex-monsieur. One let the body slide to the ground, took a look at the secret combination and showed with a quick manipulation that it wasn't so secret. In the inside compartment, nine hundred fifty thousand francs in a packet and a stamped envelope ready to be sent to the Préfecture of Paris. He put these things in his pocket and closed the briefcase carefully. Only twenty-eight seconds had passed since the action began, and the Director was still saying *allô, allô* into the ears of a cadaver. From that moment on, Zero was zero, and One left, without looking around, following instructions, to go back to the crummy hostel he'd been assigned, to wait for somebody to knock on the door, come in, kill him, and take the two envelopes. In fact, at that moment, somebody had put the address of the hostel and the number of One's room in the slot with Two's key.

VI (2)

There were two soft taps, and One said *Entrez!* in French without thinking. He was curious to know who his contact was, and he was especially eager to get the francs that made up his generous salary. He got off the bed and had time to see that whoever it was couldn't get in because the door was locked. He went to open it and had time to see that Two, who he didn't know was Two, was smiling and gesturing to be let in.

"I'm Charles Beaudelaire," he said

One took off the chain and Two, after coming in and shutting the door, stood there waiting. One understood, went over to his suitcase and took out the two envelopes.

"Do you have a cigarette?" he asked.

Two said, Yeah, sure, took out a half-empty pack and offered his victim a cigarette. He even lit it for him. While One was enjoying the last few puffs of his life, Two ripped the two envelopes open, which One didn't think was right, and looked at what was in them. He made a face that meant Yes, that's fine, put his hand in his pocket, took out the pistol and made it go poc!, even cleaner than the way One had done it. What a waste of a cigarette.

VII (3)

He was getting to the end. While he was handing over the new packet with the money and the secrets and the new address, also in Paris, to the hotel mail service, he made a quick assessment of the desk clerk, who was older than the ones at the main desk. He whispered his request into his ear and the man nodded his head: taken care of, he meant. Just wait in your room. Two felt a prickling of desire as he went up to wait, and he stretched out on the bed, as One had done while waiting for someone to kill him. To fill the time, he felt around in his shirt pocket. The last cigarette. He wondered if he should run out and buy some or... No. And he lit it and told himself he'd better enjoy it because he didn't know when he was going to be able to go out and buy more. He heard the knock, and to tempt fate a little he said, *Entrez!*, because the door wasn't locked. Damn. What a drag. It was the maid, who showed her gold tooth and pointed to the minibar:

"I have to check the drinks. I thought nobody was here."

"*Entrez, entrez,*" he said, resigned. And he pointed to the little bottles of whisky and held up three fingers, even though he was Two.

The maid didn't protest, strangely enough, put three little bottles on the table, filled the minibar with other drinks, showed her nice solid ass and left right away with one last golden smile for Two. It was only a few seconds later when there was another knock at the door.

It was a tall woman with black hair and... He'd seen her and couldn't remember where. Oh, yeah.

"Come on in."

Now he remembered. He'd seen her last night in the dining room. So basically she worked this hotel. She was really very pretty.

He sat up in bed, put out the cigarette and helped her out of the tiny jacket she was wearing. Without asking her if she wanted a drink, he made two whiskies on the rocks and thought of her nude. He smiled happily.

"What's your name?"

"Katty."

"Here."

She took the glass obediently, took a sip for his benefit and smiled. She obviously wanted to get down to work. But he wasn't in any hurry. So, he pointed to her purse:

"Hey, do you have any cigarettes?"

"I don't smoke."

"Well, it doesn't matter."

Two was very sure of himself with a pistol in his hand. But other times he was all thumbs. He had a good time anyway, didn't want to know how it was for her, and afterwards they lay there for a while, nude, quiet, remembering and dreaming. Then Two couldn't stand it any more and said, Wait, I'll be right back.

"Now where are you going?"

"For cigarettes. It'll just take a minute. I saw a machine right out..."

But he was already out of the room, barefoot, wearing only his pajama bottoms and a t-shirt, with a handful of change. Katty, from the bed, made a face to show how she felt about people who just had to smoke. Two didn't see it because he was at the other end of the hall fumbling with the coins, because he never knew which was which. Okay, how about some of these light American ones, since they don't have anything else that... That's cutting it close. Hard to believe that the change he'd grabbed was exactly enough. When he'd put in the last coin, and before he pressed the button to make the pack drop, something threw him against the machine. A few seconds later he heard a deafening noise. He looked over his shoulder, afraid, but could see only smoke, though he understood exactly what had happened. Two ran away, down the stairs, and when he realized what he was doing, he was already out on the street in a city he didn't know, wearing pajama bottoms, barefoot, and with no cigarrettes. The explosion that had destroyed his future, the refrigerator, the room and Katty, hadn't gone poc but boom.

THE TRACE

If man is five, then, the devil is six,
and if the devil is six, then, God is seven.
This monkey is gone to heaven.
Black Francis

I 'd never felt so desolate as at that very important moment in
my life when the subway train had racketed down the tunnel
and the passengers had made for the exit like nervous ants, and
I was alone on the platform in Majorstuen station with nobody
around me, and I started to hear somebody whistling. At first I
didn't catch it, but pretty soon I recognized one of the themes from
Finlandia, by Sibelius. Sibelius in the subway? Whistled? I took the
first exit, the ant one. Nothing, completely empty. Just those white
tiles, like in a bathroom, in a pointlessly lighted tunnel. Where was
the music coming from? I took a few steps, completely forgetting
that I had an appointment in ten minutes for the interview
that was supposed to get my life on track, if that was possible.
Three years ago I'd run away from home when I realized that if
I didn't do something about it, in a week I was going to marry a
woman who didn't give a shit about me. I got on a train, holding
my breath, without looking back, without even thinking about
my mother, and when I let out my breath I was in Copenhagen
feeling envious of how organized those people were and learning
first-hand all about the high cost of living. Maybe that's why I
took the ferry to Norway, I don't know. I had to get away, friends,

far away from complaints and curses from the family and from Sonia. Norway. The first taste was Oslo. I got off the ferry, found a very expensive and crummy hostel in the center of town, and have stayed there ever since. It's not easy to arrive in Oslo without knowing a word of Norwegian, or Danish, or Swedish, or English. You feel like retreating into your shell. In other words, I had to live off charming smiles and a kind of Latin-lover thing that a lot of women seem to like. And a lot of men. Two months washing dishes in a Pizza Hut and then three months as a cook's helper in a sort of Italian restaurant. I didn't do it for the money. I did it to keep from retreating into my shell. After those jobs I spoke really bad Norwegian, which made the natives like me even more.

Norwegians are really something, friends. They're innocent in this kind of charming way. They think everybody's like them. They believe that nobody would ever invade anybody else's privacy, or harm his neighbor. They hadn't met me. It's not that I'm dishonest, but if I see thirty purses lying around in the entrance to the Munch museet, full of wallets and IDs and keys just crying out to change hands, first I think, Don't do it, Quiquín. And I don't. But, come on, you see the purses every day, and every day you think, Don't do it, until finally you've had enough and one day I did it and found out that stealing, in Norway, is a piece of cake. I didn't steal for the money; let's say I did it for art's sake, to get inside those Norwegian heads, where their brains are half frozen from living so far up north.

And, hey, how about the day that Pere Bros, that ass kisser, came to the Universitetets Aula, just before he packed it in? He did the Spring (saccharine), the Kreutzer (self-indulgent) and the Franck (perfect), with that idiot Gidon Kremer on the violin, and I made out like a bandit. Literally, friends. Because the Norwegians are so Norwegian that instead of a cloakroom, the Universitetets Aula just has some hooks in the hall. I'm not kidding, friends. So they can't complain, because when Kremer and Bros were working their way through the andante of the opus 24, I said to myself, Quiquín, go take a piss because this is getting boring. So I go out and there's all these coats saying, Come on, Quiquín, do it. I went back in the middle of the Kreutzer happy, because when it comes to providing employment to thieves, the Norwegians are real professionals.

I didn't spend a single night, friends, thinking about home. Despite the fact that my mother would still send me money every month, on the sly. Mother love. Even my father didn't know I was in Oslo. One day I called home when I knew my mother would be alone, and described as much of my life as I could and asked for my allowance, as if I were still in Barcelona. I said I had to go to concerts and live, I don't know, like an educated person. Pretending to cry when she asked me why I'd left Sonia when the Quadras were such nice people was probably a bit much. But what was I supposed to say? Was I supposed to say, Mother, I don't want to marry somebody who laughs at me because my thing is too little? Was I supposed to say, Mother, I don't want to marry a pig who says she doesn't like the Stones or Jethro Tull or Monteverdi or any kind of music? Crying was the best option. Well done, Quiquín, because since we had that awful conversation, Mother puts out every month. Result: I allow myself, once in a while, to think about my mother. And only about my mother. Because if I start remembering Sonia or my father or the rest of the family, if they show up in my head all by themselves, I just look north, as if threatening to go to Lapland or even the North Pole to freeze out those family memories forever. This tunnel had a bend at the end where maybe... No: at the end the same antiseptic white tiles all lined up with nobody there. Brad Pitt was looking scornfully down from a billboard and refusing to tell me where the mysterious music was coming from, but Sibelius sounded the same, neither closer nor farther away, down there in the subway. Next to Brad Pitt, a picture of a beach that could've been Salou informed the citizens of Oslo that Israel was the perfect place for a vacation, with personal safety absolutely guaranteed by the trademark Israeli efficiency. I took a good look, because it really did look like Salou. You could practically see the Segarra tower! Can you imagine passing Salou off as Israel? According to those swindlers, Salou was a charming Israeli tourist town called Dor, with little boats, nets, happy fishermen, starfish and a casino. Beautiful scenery, beaches, a port where the environment and its traditional fisheries and gastronomy strill thrive. Discover the friendly face of Israel. You'll love it. I turned away from this fraud and found myself on the same platform where I'd gotten off. Finlandia was still bouncing off the tiles, almost mockingly. Until the arrival of another train covered up all the melodies in the world, and the doors opened to vomit out a hundred imprisoned citizens who, probably, couldn't care less about Sibelius. It isn't that I was particularly interested in Sibelius; it's that I have a musical gift that's a pain in the ass: I hear any kind of music and I absolutely have to listen to it. And I memorize it and remember it forever and ever. There's too much music inside of me, and I try to keep it confined to my stomach. But when it decides to play inside my head, there's nothing I can do except go crazy. So I waited until the station emptied out, but then the enfuriating thing was that the music was gone. It seemed like, I'm not completely sure, but it seemed like in some rugged corner of that labyrinth somebody, like the Phantom of the Opera, was stifling a snicker. My mind was so far away with that shadowy apparition that I wasn't even shocked when I looked at my watch: I was already shamelessly late for my interview with Dr. Werenskiold, friends, and there I was thinking about Sibelius deep underground. Half confused, half embarrassed by the snicker but not by being late, I headed for the exit and the government building where I was supposed to find the solution to all of my material and spititual problems. I'm not kidding, friends, I felt like strangling that snickerer.

Outside, even though it was August, it was goddam cold. Looking at the huge ministry building made me feel very small. It made the same impression on me that, in more magical times, cathedrals had made on the faithful. Or the paralyzing feeling that I'd had when I went to the Nasjonalgalleriet (four purses plundered, 380 crowns, a very nice tamagochi with whose interior I became quite intimate, and three drivers' licenses that turned into kroner a few days later) to look at paintings. I was particularly impressed by a non-painting. In gallery 34, and I'll always remember that it was gallery 34 because I could hear through the window that faced the street, rising up like sour and unwanted bile, the disgusting sarabande from Bach's second partita played on a violin with an out-of-tune D string. I was about to demand that the woman who was the guard for galleries 30 to 36 explain why such sounds were allowed to penetrate that temple. But I didn't do it; I just gave her a dirty look and she smiled back. It was that Latin lover thing again. Gallery 34 and the non-painting. I stood for half an hour in front of an undirty shadow on the wall behind a not-very-large painting by Rembrandt van Rijn, which was traveling around Europe somewhere. Contemplating a non-painting is good for your soul. The difference in tone between the wall ad usum and the patch of wall that was protected for years by Rembrandt reveals the passage of time, the tempus fugit, the tempus edax rerum, the glances of many, many pasty Norwegians, fumes from the street that have stuck to the wall like onion skin – if any Norwegian car or Norwegian furnace produces fumes, which I doubt. The wall was greenish, completely unartistic. In contrast, the color of the hidden and now uncovered wall was brave, vivid, a little lighter, optimistic, kind of Stand aside, it's my turn. And the line, the border between the two greens showed the exact outline of the Rembrandt. Bravo. Magnificent. I don't remember the paintings that were on either side of the non-painting by Rembrandt. After this fabulous experience, I went to every museum in Oslo looking for more non-paintings. I found three or four that made me very happy.

As I entered the huge lobby of the ministry with all of its escalators, the air conditioning took my breath away, because the Norwegians think that if the sun's out it must be sweltering. After consulting with the bored civil servant who was directing traffic, I headed for the longest escalator. The one next to it was going down, so that the citizens who were on their way out, satisfied or mortified, passed by me. That's when I saw her.

I could care less about Norway. It's been a tool, that's all. The thing is, my friends, that to keep from having to go back to Barcelona, it was a good idea to become a Norwegian citizen.

Especially if my mother kept putting out. And Dr. Werenskiold was the man who had to decide, after a number of complaints from citizens who were unjustly irritated with me, what to do with the charming Quiquín. Because even if I could care less about Norway, I want to stay here. I just went into business with this Bosnian hardass, smuggling cigarrettes, and we could get so rich that it makes me dizzy just to think about it. And then, with my shorts full of thousand-crown bills, Sonia wouldn't say it was little.

And there in the lobby of the ministry I saw her for the first time in my life. She was coming towards me, as I was going towards her, on the magic belt of the escalator, and she looked at me with glade-colored eyes and let her hair fly, just for me, as if she were on a magic carpet. She had on a short dress, very simple, that set off but did not misrepresent her perfect figure. And she was looking at me, friends, with the same intensity with which I was examining her, amazed. The first Norwegian I was really attracted to. What a woman. What a goddess. Until we were next to one another and immobile, we passed one another by; and that was when I sensed the fragrance of her perfume, her skin, her clothes, and the subtle aroma of her memories. A fleeting sensation, a couple of seconds, but it's lasted all my life. I didn't see if there were other people on the down escalator or if the goddess was by herself. I fell, open-mouthed in admiration, possessed by that urgent call, as I flew up the stairs in search of the decidedly un-epic Dr. Werenskiold, who'd been drumming his fingers on the table for the last quarter of an hour and thinking bad thoughts about me, because this was the last and definitive meeting. She'd turned too and was looking at me with the same intensity, it seemed, as I was looking at her. She looked like a valkyrie. And both of us experienced that irreproducible sensation of knowing we were alone in the world, with no thieves, no Norwegians, no bad guys to hurt us, no witches, no boring arguments, no cruel Sonias. And because both of us had the same feeling at the same time, we had the same idea, and at the end of the escalator, I was about to go down and she to come up. I'm impulsive and I didn't realize how ridiculous it would have been if we'd passed one another again in the same place. But she, who's Norwegian, was the smart one, because she stopped and got off the escalator. She waited for me, as faithful as Penelope, for all the days, months and years it took for me to go down, friends, surrounded by all those people that didn't matter to us. Once we were face to face, I could see that she was tall, maybe a few inches taller than me, and that she did indeed have eyes the color of a river glade in which, if I wasn't careful, I could drown. I smiled and said, My name is Abelard. What's yours?

"I finally found you."

We stepped into a corner and she ran her fingertips over my hand as she repeated, Abelard, as if trying out a new name on a new person, and she seemed to think it was fine.

"You're gorgeous."

"Have you had the interview with Dr. Werenskiold?"

"Sure! Norway is huge, but I knew I'd end up finding you."

She smiled and pointed at my face as if to say that she'd never seen eyes like that. With her velvet voice, coming up close:

"I can't do anything else for you, Mr. Masdexaxart. It's up to the Ministry."

"I've never seen anything like yours either." I grabbed her tenderly by the arms. "You're the most important thing that's ever happened to me. Why haven't we ever met before?"

"If you don't let go of me, I'm going to have to call the police, even if I am your lawyer."

"Don't, I'm not Italian," I said ungraciously, letting her go, a little confused.

"It might be a week before they decide. I'll be there."

"It's not necessary."

"I know you speak Norwegian very well, but if you want..."

"Thank you," I interrupted her. "You speak it very well too." And I brought the conversation back to basics . "It doesn't matter where I'm from."

She probably thought it was stupid of me to turn my back on my roots, because she did nothing but cast her eyes serenely downward. I felt afraid and loved her even more. Of course it's important if it's important to her! So why the hell wasn't I Italian?

Why did I have to be born in Barcelona? I damned my father and mother to hell (no, not my mother, I saved her right away) for not having had me in Montescaglioso. I was so deeply in love with the valkyrie for so many centuries that I forgot all about the Italian problem. I took her hand and let go of it right away, because it was burning, and she touched my skin again, as if tasting it, with the tips of her fingers. And she smiled:

"There are going to be some problems." In a lower voice, "Your case isn't simple. They even want to bring in the medical records."

"With you by my side I do not fear the night, Lord."

"Come on, you can share my taxi if you want."

I was in the presence of happiness and I was drinking it in through my pores. Now I understood why fate hadn't let me stop, on my flight through the desert, until I got to Oslo, the city of peace and joy. Isolde was waiting for me.

"Take me into your bed, Goddess."

I helped her out a little, because she'd gone quiet, with her mouth open, virginal, reticent and shy.

"Fine, Eloisa. You know where we can go on vacation?"

"The taxis are through that door."

"Dor. It's a quiet Israeli village, next to Salou, 500 kilometers north of Tel Aviv and twenty kilometers south of Haifa. Beautiful scenery, beaches, a port where the environment and its traditional fisheries and gastronomy strill thrive. Discover the friendly face of Israel. You'll love it. Shall I reserve two seats on El Al? We can spend the next millennium there."

She was listening intently and I tried to be sincere.

"Okay," I said. "We can go to Dor after they finally make me a Norwegian."

Then I had a brief vision of Dr. Werenskiold signing the papers and granting me a passport, and years of life in Norway in peace and harmony by the side of my valkyrie. All of a sudden, my blood ran cold: that bastard Werenskiold! He hadn't signed anything yet! And I started to sweat.

"You're going to have to wait a minute, Eloisa. I forgot I have to be somewhere."

"Didn't you say…"

"It'll just take a minute," I interrupted her. "Will you wait for me?"

And I was rude enough to look at my watch. She nodded as if to say, What choice do I have? and watched me walk away. I didn't realize until much later that the color of the water in the glade had gone cloudy. Fervent as a medieval knight, I ran up the stairs, pushing aside the poor devils who didn't know Eloisa and rushing to make it to the doctor, to meekly accept the conditions for changing my nationality and sign on the dotted line, get the thing over with and go back to happiness.

Things never turn out the way you want. Not even in Norway. Dr. Werenskiold didn't know the valkyrie Eloisa was waiting for me at the foot of the ministry-mountain with her glade-like eyes, did you, Dr. Werenskiold? So he made me wait seven confusing and humiliating minutes. One, two, three, four, five, six, seven indecent minutes that could separate me from my eternal love. And afterwards, when I was sitting in front of him with my flattering Latin smile, the doctor spent two hours cleaning his glasses and looking at me in silence, making the same face that my father makes to mean, What are we going to do with this boy, Mother, what are we going to do? I'm not going to give you a car or a horse or a shotgun; you don't deserve them. My father has always treated me as if I weren't a human being… Enough of that, it makes me sick and I don't want to throw up.

"We still can't say that you have a regular job, Mr. Masdexaxart."

Fine. Tatoo the serial number on my arm. Long live Norway. I'm in a hurry. I have to go.

"But I have a steady income."

"I'm talking about work, Mr. Masdexaxart."

If there weren't so many people around, I'd take this letter opener and stick it in your fat priest's neck. I want to be Norwegian because I love Eloisa, period.

"I have an interview tomorrow: home appliance repair."

"Well…" Half an hour's thought. "That might be right for you."

I like to tell lies, doctor. Especially if people are going to believe them.

"Ubi bene, ibi patria."

"What?" The priest was suspicious, in case it was a secret message.

"I mean I love Norway with all my heart, Dr. Werenskiold."

"I'm not saying you don't, but there seem to be a lot of citizens who aren't very fond of you. You owe three months' rent and there are now sixteen official complaints about your behavior."

Assholes, unemployed Norwegians who want to give me a hard time because I'm not blond or tall and my thing is little.

"I'm sure it's a misunderstanding, Dr. Werenskiold."

"Sixteen misunderstandings."

The doctor's irony was insulting. But he was playing at home, and I couldn't give in to the taunts of the crowd. I smiled, in other words, and because I was like a love token in the hands of fate, friends, that wanted only to return to my glade, I gave up on the interview.

When I headed for the lobby, I was about to shout that I was the happiest man in the world. There was a crowd of people and nobody could get to the escalator. So I stuck my head up in the direction of the blessed wall where she was waiting for me and put on a smile a perfect happiness. But after a few seconds my smile melted. Eloisa wasn't there. Okay, she had to be... Maybe over there... Maybe she was looking for somewhere to throw... Or she'd gone out to see if... By the time I got to the lobby I'd invented two thousand plausible explanations for Eloisa's disappearance. I looked around: lots of indifferent faces, but the countenance of my valkyrie was not among them. Then I felt afraid and my soul said, Eloisa, my glade, ubi es?

I don't know if it took two or three hours, but I looked everywhere. Everywhere. I asked hundreds of people, I went out on the street fifty times thinking, Shit, shit, shit, what if somebody's run over her, or kidnapped her, or simply killed her. I checked the neighborhood, I went through everything, even the trashcans, looking for any sign of the girl with the river-glade eyes. But the world had ended and the evidence pointed to my never seeing Eloisa again. In the middle of the afternoon, tired, famished, sweaty and parched, I left the Ministry wanting only to get inside the deafening world of King Crimson so they could blow you all away. Not you, friends: them. And I wanted some Crim so bad that I thought the best thing would be to go to the little record store on Osterhausgate and act like I wanted to buy *In the Wake of Poseidon*, for example. And after an hour, smile my Mediterranean smile and tell the Sigrid on duty, No, I guess not. I went down into the metro wondering if the store on Osterhausgate was the best place to listen to Crim and forget about my problems. In spite of everything, the white tiles in the tunnel reminded me of the hidden melody from a few hours before, and all of a sudden I was done with Crimson and wanted a quick dose of Sibelius. I was sad, friends. Very sad. Quae solitudo esset in Metropolitano, quae vastitas! As Saint Stephen, the first martyr, exclaimed in a situation similar to mine. I let three trains go by hoping to be able to hear the whistled music in that impossible place, but, no luck. Worse, an imposing-looking woman with black hair and blue eyes set up a speaker and a diabolical machine right next to me, threatened me with a smile and started singing, to a taped accompaniment, an ignominious selection of the best known and most strenuous arias from the operatic repertory. While the fake soprano filled the air with arias, I was trying to decide whether to crack open her skull or cut her vocal cords. But I remembered that I was playing away from home, and chose to abstain. When I'd had enough, I decided to get away on the first train that came by. As soon as the train arrived, the woman fell silent in honor of my departure. The car was almost empty. Just as the doors were closing behind me with a sigh, I heard the same melody from *Finlandia*, clear, precise and almost mocking. It came from the platform. I tried desperately to keep the doors from closing by trying to stick my hand between them, but, indifferent, they guillotined my plea as the train started up, and against my will I left all my hopes and dreams behind.

When I got to my hostel, I, Quiquín of Barcelona, had fallen from my horse in Osterhausgate. The Sigrid on duty was going to give me *Poseidon*, but there on the counter was a pile of *The Last Recital of Pere Bros* and that made me wonder because if it really was his last recital then he must've checked out, and it wasn't very long ago that he and Kremer had made me rich in Oslo. I was curious and asked to listen to the disc. Schubert, as usual, crying in B-flat major. But that damn what's his name, Fischer. That's one weird, Fripp thing. So I put it on five times and I decided to steal one of the CDs because it was only right that I should have that fantastic music. Coming back from my Damascus with the CD in the pocket of my jacket, I found a smiling Dr. Werenskiold outside of my hostel flanked by two hefty uniformed civil servants. He asked me where on earth I'd been all that time and informed me that he was then turning me over to one of the gorillas, who was in fact a fairly well-known police commissioner whose name I couldn't remember. It seems that my lawyer had filed a complaint against me for attempted valkyrie abuse and my hardass Bosnian friend had given evidence that I was the head of an illegal web of distribution of contraband tobacco. Both of these outrageous lies made me angry, but the friendly civil servants made a gesture that meant, Don't even try.

If I'd been able to write all this down, friends, it would have been the First Letter of Quiquín to the Barcelonans. But I can't, because the police van is bouncing around in a very un-Norwegian way. Enough dreaming, Quiquín, you need to start thinking in practical terms. Right now I'm going to tell these Vikings stuffed with milk and cheese that I won't make any statement unless my mother is present.

NEGOTIATION

That's when he knew he was getting old, when he noticed the fine lines that had begun to chisel the passage of time into Yves Saulnier's face, giving it a vague air of fatigue. They sat down around the table in silence, the lawyers for the other side dressed impeccably in gray, as expectant as Monsignor Walzer, looking from him to Mr. Saulnier, probably amazed. The Vatican lawyer, Lambertini, who was wearing not gray but even more proper black and had been the first to take a seat, was the only one who wasn´t looking nervously around. He closed his eyes as if getting ready to pray. Or to take a nap.

"It is my duty," Yves Saulnier said in a hard voice, "to protest in the strongest possible terms what can only be considered a slander on the part of the Church."

Monsignor Gaus looked straight at Saulnier and paused a long time before responding, as if he too had fallen asleep, like his lawyer.

"You may not know," he said when he woke up, "but it is not slanderous. It's an accusation based on evidence."

"We're prepared to take this to court," said the Vatican lawyer, emerging from sleep, "as far as we have to go." And he returned to his Nirvana-like state.

"Where is this evidence?"

"If Mr. Pierre Grossman doesn't want to settle, the evidence will go to court."

Saulnier leapt from his seat, indignant.

"You're bluffing!"

Monsignor Gaus stood up, imitating the other's outburst.

"Fine, we'll take it to court." Coldly, "Gentlemen..."

"I'm not authorized to..." On his feet, Saulnier wanted more time. "I need proof that you're not lying to me."

Monsignor Gaus thought for a few seconds. He picked up a piece of paper and wrote a few words on it with his fountain pen. He blew lightly on the paper, folded it and handed it to the person next to him. The paper went from hand to hand, carefully folded, until it got to Saulnier. He sat down, unfolded the paper, read it and looked down the table, perplexed. Monsignor Gaus was amused by his expression. He answered the question that Saulnier hadn't yet asked.

"Monsieur Piere Grossman will understand it."

"I should... ," said Saulnier, looking from side to side.

Monsignor Gaus lifted his anointed hands in a very liturgical gesture that meant, Go right ahead, feel free. He pressed a button and immediately an attendant came in to usher Saulnier and his two lawyers through a side door that led to a discreet office. The two monsignors and the laconic lawyer were silent, motionless, prepared to wait. All of a sudden, Monsignor Gaus pointed to the telephone.

"I want to hear the conversation with Grossman."

They're not that stupid," answered Monsignor Walzer. "They'll use their cell phones."

"Maybe not." Authoritarian: "Let's see."

Monsignor Walzer got up somewhat unwillingly and went to the telephone. He pressed a button and said in a low, cautious voice, "See if you can connect me with the outside office. Just to listen."

In a few seconds he hung up and turned to his superior without trying to hide his satisfaction.

"They're not using the Vatican phones."

"Grossman won't agree to anything by phone," said Lambertini, opening his eyes and looking at one of the empty chairs. "He'll only say yes or no."

"He'll say yes," said Monsignor Gaus.

Walzer couldn't keep from saying, "What did you write on that paper?"

Monsignor smiled and acted as if he hadn't noticed his subordinate´s impertinence. To get out of an uncomfortable situation, Walzer went on the attack.

"It seems that you'd rather negotiate with criminals than turn them in."

"It seems that it's not a good idea to have enemies."

Neither of them saw the lawyer, who seemed to be in a world of his own, assent with an imperceptible nod of his head.

"Negotiating with thieves is stealing," insisted Walzer.

"Monsignor Walzer..." Now Gaus looked him in the eye as coldly as he could. "Enough of that tone, we're not children."

The impassive lawyer made a minimal gesture that meant he'd liked the response. Walzer, in contrast, was motionless, his mouth open in surprise. He continued in the same tone.

"If you've found some weak spot, whatever it is, now is the time to destroy them. As you did with Umberto de Luca."

"Umberto wasn't an enemy."

"But you ruined him."

"To avoid a major scandal."

Lambertini had nodded off again. Monsignor Walzer raised a finger in vindication.

"Fine, I agree. But these people are enemies."

"If you crowd your prey, you'll get hurt when they try to run."

"How can you let criminals go free?" And as if he couldn't think of a better argument: "Render unto Caesar that which is Caesar's and unto God..."

"Monsignor," Monsignor Gaus cut him off, curt, harsh, fed up, "if you want to learn how to negotiate when there are millions at stake, keep your mouth shut and your morality up your ass."

Bright red, Monsignor Walzer opened his briefcase and started to rummage around in it as if searching for his lost principles.

After six minutes of leaden silence, the three negotiators came back into the room. Saulnier, struggling to seem relaxed, sat down and said, "All right. Monsieur Grossman agrees to negotiate."

"So now you call yourself Yves Saulnier."

"And you, Monsignor."

"Don't forget that I'm a bishop."

"I don't control this thing. I swear by your holy balls that I'm not in charge here."

"I'm sorry, but I have to do my duty."

"I should have killed you."

"What kind of mess have you gotten yourself into, Monsieur Saulnier?"

They stopped talking because the waiter was taking away their plates after having looked first at one of them and then at the other.

"What do zero, one, two and three mean?"

"If you think I'm going to explain that to you now, you're crazy."

"How do you expect me to... I heve no power to negotiate if I don't know the reason why Grossman..."

"The only thing you have to negotiate with me is how you're going to give the stolen paintings back to the Church."

Saulnier smiled at the waiter who was serving hake and potatoes, which looked excellent. When he'd gone away, Saulnier leaned over his plate and said quietly, "If I'm the one to blame for coming out on the losing end of these conversations, I could be killed."

Silence. The hake was getting cold. Hake with spring garlic and perfect tiny potatoes that smelled delicious. Now they didn't look at one another. A lot of time's gone by, there's a lot of distance between us, and you're in a business where you have to risk your neck.

Yves Saulnier gestured to the monsignor to begin. He set a good example by starting to eat, as if he hadn't just said, I could be killed. But the monsignor had lost his appetite. He put down his silverware and looked at the other man.

"You're going to lose. But I'm sure you'll land on your feet."

"What does zero, one, two, three mean?"

"I can't tell you."

"That's shit. You can tell me everything."

"We're playing on opposite teams. How is it that of the twenty-six paintings in the traveling show, the thieves took only the three that the Church had in storage in Oslo?"

"That's obvious. They were far and away the most valuable."

The monsignor took a bite of fish and chewed it unenthusiastically.

"Would they really kill you?"

"We can help each other. What does zero, one, two, three mean?"

"You want Grossman by the balls, don't you?"

Saulnier smiled, his fork in the air. He went back to eating. Monsignor Gaus made sure there was no waiter hanging around and took an envelope out of the pocket of his jacket. He put it in front of Saulnier, who wiped his lips with his napkin, put it on the table, and extended his fingers towards the envelope. He opened it and took out some photos. Four photos. When he realized what they showed, he quickly put them back in the envelope so that no wandering eye could see what it shouldn't see. It seemed to Monsignor Gaus that Saulnier had turned a little pale. Saulnier put the envelope in his pocket. He let a few seconds go by. Obviously, he was impressed by what he'd seen. A thousand centuries later, tapping his pocket, he said, "How do you know? How do you know that's him?"

Surprisingly, the negotiations were finalized in the offices of the Musei e Gallerie more rapidly than anyone expected. The celebration was in the Santa Clara salon. Cardinal Grimaldi, of the

Pia Instituzione, radiated happiness as he made small talk, killing time, with the two notaries; the one hired by the Nasjonalgalleriet of Oslo and agreed to by the Vatican and the chief notary of Vatican City. When he saw Monsignor Gaus come in, impassive, escorted by a mute Walzer and a silent Lambertini, the cardinal went to embrace him. I haven't been this happy in eighteen years, he said. Gaus calculated that it must have been eighteen years ago when the Holy Father had told him he was making him a prince of the Church. Cardinal Grimaldi offered conventional congratulations to the other members of the team and they all fell silent. The ceremony had to be brief because the pianist who'd been hired to play some Chopin and things like that had tragically and unilaterally annuled the contract, despite having collected a five percent advance. The act itself was over in no time, because it consisted of nothing more than the Norwegian notary and the chief notary certifying that three works had been returned to their legal owners: Pintoricchio's *The Coronation of the Virgin*, Caravaggio's *The Descent from the Cross* and Rembrandt's *The Philosopher*, the most emblematic of the three because of its incalculable value if it were ever to reach the illegal market. A week earlier, the Vatican's experts had certified both their authenticity and their perfect condition.

"Monsignor," His Eminence confessed, "if it weren't for the fact that we have no interest in material gain, I'd be tempted to see to it that you were well rewarded for your intervention on behalf of the coffers of the Vatican."

Monsignor Gaus bowed his head, humbly. It was inappropriate to speak of compensation. But he discreetly suggested to the cardinal that he might think of granting a promotion to his lay colleague, Lambertini, or adding a bonus to his fee.

He'd never been in the presence of Pierre Grossman. He'd never even seen a picture of him. Pierre Grossman was discretion personified. One of the richest men in Europe, he lived in a kind of voluntary exile, dedicated to the preservation of his fortune and the supervision of the many businesses that made it possible, and to paying the losses occasioned by his wife's passion, a management agency that she managed very badly.

He hadn't imagined him like this. Grossman was wearing a jacket of a strange reddish color, which didn't look bad on him. He wore his white hair very short and the skin of his face wasn't tanned by the sun or the snow, but unevenly pale. It was impossible to tell how old he was.

They were in a suite in a Geneva hotel that had been decorated in a hurry. Unaccompanied, one on either side of the table, they sat at the same time. The monsignor wanted to spend as little time as possible across from that man whose eyes he found it hard to meet, because they bored into him like diamond drills. So, he got down to business and took out the envelope. Grossman took it and removed the photos, without bothering to hide them. He looked at them one by one, impassive, without showing any emotion.

"The negatives?"

"They're in the envelope. But these days that doesn't mean anything."

"So what do you suggest?"

"I'll consider the whole matter of the photos to be a secret of the confessional."

"I don't give a damn about your secret of the confessional, Monsignor."

"I'm a priest. You must know what the term implies."

"I blow your secrets of the confessional," now he was looking him patiently in the eye, "out my ass. Can I say it any plainer than that?"

"Then you can just go ahead and kill me now."

"How many people know?"

"The detective I hired and I myself."

"Who's the detective?"

"He's dead."

"How do I know he's really dead?"

"There's proof. A gas explosion in the hotel where he was staying." He passed him a sheet of paper. "Here's the information."

Pierre Grossman took the paper, looked over it calmly, folded it and put it in his pocket.

"Nobody else?" he said.

"Nobody else."

They didn't shake hands or say goodbye. They simply parted forever. Geneva was freezing and the monsignor, who had no desire to play tourist, went back to the Vatican immediately. In any case, he had a good reason for not staying away from home too long.

The entire room was dominated by dark ochres and a wonderful light, on the right, which was a splash of sun against the window. How I would have liked to be that peaceful man who spends his days reading, studying, wondering and thinking, now about God, now about the big questions, the Gran Interrogatori, who am I, where did I come from, where am I going. And after a frugal repast, to return to the books and learn the wisdom hidden there and be a small lantern, small but a lantern, to light the way of the Church. How I would like that. Instead I've been called to watch over the Church's material goods, I can rarely have a frugal meal, I can never while away the time with a good, fat book in my hands, and I'm not happy. My God, how I would like to be that philosopher.

Because Monsignor Gaus couldn't be that, he had to be content with having the painting hanging on the wall of his private gallery. For the first month, the monsignor spent a good hour every day sitting there, in front of the Rembrandt, looking at all of its details, trying to breathe in the the odor of some brush stroke snuffed out by the passage of time. Next to the Rembrandt, on the same panel of the wall, hung Leonardo's unfinished *Saint Jerome*. And in the same room, but on the opposite wall, Modest Urgell's *The Cemetery*, a huge, melancholy, perfect work, which he hadn't tired of loving since it disappeared for a few months from the Museu Dalí fifteen years ago. In the other room, the king of the paintings was Fra Filippo Lippi's *The Coronation of the Virgin*, a charmer with colors that were somewhat dark but extraordinarily warm. He breathed in, full, satisfied, almost happy, for on his walls rested some of his great and eternal loves. He couldn't maintain this pleasurable state for long, because the bell rang three times—which called up a vague and distant memory.

Yves Saulnier went into the book-filled library room and waited patiently for the monsignor to return with a tray of coffee so steamily aromatic that it was entrancing. After the first sip, he took the envelope out of his pocket and put it on the coffee table.

"This is yours," he said.

Monsignor Gaus picked it up and checked the contents. The first photo, the most horrifying, showed a baby in a crib with its face destroyed from a bullet shot at close range. A little puff of sky-blue smoke was the sole, useless witness to that horrible crime. The monsignor forced himself to look at all of them, despite their rawness. Two more photos of the child and then one presumably of the mother, sitting on a sofa with her head thrown back and her mouth destroyed, also by a bullet. The mother in a housecoat. In her lap, a pretty and hopeful bouquet of flowers that she was holding in her clenched, dead hands. And two or three other photos showing details of that horrifying double murder carried out in a room in a maternity clinic.

"Everything's there."

"Watch out for Grossman. He doesn't know you know. He doesn't know you've seen this."

"That's best. Just in case." Saulnier took a sip of coffee, made a discreet gesture to ask for permission to light a cigarette, and leaned back on the sofa.

"How is it," he asked, "that I work for Pierre Grossman and I had no idea about this aspect of your... activities, but you...?"

"I've always been more clever than you."

The monsignor put the photos back in the envelope and gave it to Saulnier.

"What do you mean?" Surprised. "I can keep them?"

"They can help you or hurt you. It depends on how you use them." He leaned towards him as if about to tell a great secret. "He who is the first to know where the river is can become the owner of the water." He smiled. "An old Hebrew saying."

Saulnier emptied the cup. It was really good. He put the little cup on the table, delicately, while he thought about rivers of water and rivers of blood. He looked the monsignor in the eye.

"What does zero, one, two, three mean?"

Monsignor Gaus, prelate of the Vatican Curia, patiently explained to Saulnier that murder for hire was an extraordinarily lucrative business, that the various agents who had to carry out the assignment without leaving a trace were known by the names Zero, One and Two, that the whole thing was very sordid and he wanted nothing to do with the places where such things were arranged. Saulnier had no sympathy for these protestations.

"You have to show me your gallery."

It was part of the agreement. Monsignor Gaus took him through the secret door and spent more than an hour showing him the paintings that only his most trusted confidants could look at. They took Saulnier's breath away.

"Won't this ever be discovered?"

"Never. As long as I'm here, I control what goes on. And when I'm not, they can come looking for me."

Saulnier stopped next to *The Philosopher* and looked at the monsignor.

"Have you ever asked yourself which of us is the original and which is the copy?"

"Mother used to say that you were older because the twin that's born first was conceived last." Monsignor smiled at the memory, and continued, "But I'm convinced that you've always been a bad copy of me."

The two negotiators embraced surrounded by all the beauty on those walls. Yves Saulnier left, carrying the photos as a passport, without turning around, knowing that it might be twenty years before they saw each other again. Monsignor Gaus, however, indulged in the weakness of watching him until he went out the door of the apartment. He finished his coffee in silence.

"If I'm not mistaken, Monsignor, the fourteen paintings in this magnificent room are all originals."

Pale at the door to his gallery, the monsignor looked at the lawyer, Lambertini, dressed in black and seated in the comfortable armchair which he usually used for looking at *The Philosopher*, and the same detective with a cigarette in his mouth who'd helped him two years ago and who, quite obviously, had not been blown to smithereens in any hotel anywhere. How the fucking hell had they gotten into his gallery? How the fucking hell did they know it existed?

Lambertini, seated and looking down, was sleeping, as usual. From the depths of his sleep he said, If it hadn't been for the invaluable help of...—he made a polite gesture in the direction of the detective—I would never have noticed that you're the one in charge of working out the details, with no witnesses, and the result is an original for you and an excellent fake for the place to which it was to be returned.

"All of this," the monsignor pointed to his collection with a trembling hand, "they're all copies."

"That's shit, Monsignor," said Lambertini without raising his voice. He waved his hand in the direction of the paintings. "They exist only so you can look at them?" And as if he could barely suppress his irritation, "It took me months of work to figure out that what's in the Gallerie are fakes."

"Would you mind leaving us alone?" said Monsignor to the Judas detective. And, ironically, "I suppose you know by now where I keep the coffee."

Lambertini nodded his head slightly towards the detective, who left the room.

Once they were alone, the monsignor sat down in the other armchair.

"I'd like to make it worth your while," he said, testing the ground.

"No. I'll turn you in if you don't kill me first."

"I'm not a murderer. What do you want? The Caravaggio?" With a pain in his heart that almost took his breath away, he continued, "Do you want the Leonardo?"

"The fakes are magnificent. How is it that the experts in the Vatican haven't..." He stopped. His eyes widened in admiration. "Of course. It's them, they make the fakes."

"This is just talk. You can't prove anything."

"I want the Rembrandt."

"What?"

Silence. It had been said. Now it was his move. He moved his king.

"No."

Lambertini moved the black queen to check. "Fine. We'll accuse you of robbery and forgery in the Italian and the Vatican courts." And with the knight and the castle in place, "The press will eat it up, Monsignor."

Monsignor took the bishop on the black square in his unsteady hand and put it in front of the king, to protect it from the faithless black queen.

"You can't do this to me, Lambertini."

He hadn't noticed where the black knight and the black castle were.

"As you wish." The lawyer stood and looked greedily at the paintings. "I'll go to court." Nodding towards the interior of the apartment, "My associate is staying here to make sure you don't do anything stupid."

"Why are you doing this to me?"

"Animam pro anima, oculum pro oculo, dentem pro dente," recited Lambertini in a deep voice.

"I don't understand."

Lambertini put a finger to his mouth and lifted his cheek to show his teeth. He pointed to a space between his molars. The only thing that occurred to the monsignor was that Lambertini, his customary good manners abandoned, was making crude gestures, and this meant things were serious.

"I still don't understand."

"In Montescaglioso we say that showing an enemy the space between your teeth indicates utter contempt."

"Why? What have I done to you?" The monsignor didn't know which piece to move.

"You had Umberto de Luca fired."

"Yes. For immorality. And why do you care about..."

"A public scandal," went on Lambertini, serious, "cruel speculation about male lovers... Umberto de Luca is ruined and contemplates suicide." The lawyer again showed the space next to his molar. "You don't know how much I hate you, Monsignor."

Monsignor Gaus got to his feet. He offered a castle.

"We can negotiate."

Lambertini made an effort to get back into the conversation, and resumed his usual cold manner of speaking.

"My negotiation is that I want the Rembrandt."

"You wouldn't know how to appreciate it."

"Don't jump to conclusions." With a polite smile, "I've learned a lot from you."

"You..."

"Look, Monsignor, even if I didn't feel like looking at the painting... knowing how much it's worth on the black market makes it even more remarkable to Umberto and me."

Monsignor moved closer to the painting, intent on resisting the assault of the black queen, the knight, the castle and now the other castle.

"Checkmate," Lambertini said softly. He signalled that the monsignor should stand aside. "I only want the Rembrandt, Monsignor." He made a slight bow. "If you crowd your prey, you'll get hurt when they try to run."

"I'm not planning to run."

"It's a saying. I hope that, starting tomorrow, we can continue to work together regularly with no hard feelings."

The armchair was where Lambertini had left it. The monsignor sat in it, forlorn. After a while he raised his head: the empty space on the wall was worse than a blow to the face. *The Philosopher* hadn't yet had time to leave a shadow on the paint. But the monsignor understood the profound sorrow that the contemplation of a non-painting could produce. He wasn't willing to accept that absence in his life. Desolate, he touched the orphaned wall. He went to the kitchen, made another aromatic coffee, the sixth, and, while he was drinking it, took out his private diary and placed a call. He waited patiently for someone to answer. After a long time, a professional-sounding voice picked up.

"I want to speak with Monsieur Grossman," the monsignor said.

WINTERREISE

I walk on snow, barefoot, my head uncovered.
Ausiàs March

Zoltán Wesselényi opened the umbrella and sheltered under it. The solitary path crunched under his feet. He began to notice the soft murmur of the rain, like tears, on the umbrella, and his backache started to act up, as it usually did when it was humid. He knew there wouldn't be anybody there but, still, he moved right along because he didn't like to arrive late. But if he knew there wouldn't be anybody there, why was his heart racing?

In the past twenty-five years he'd been tempted to make this visit a dozen times. He'd never had the heart. He knew that near Schubert's tomb he would have found only Japanese tourists, photographing one another in groups of ten around the monument to Mozart, panning the whole area with their video cameras and running off, urged on by the guide, because the *choucroute* would be ready at seven. Nobody had told them that Wolf was behind Beethoven and beyond the Strausses was Schönberg.

When he got to the tomb of Alois Liechtenstein, his heart was pounding, and not because he'd been hurrying but because there was a remote possibility that he was coming to the end of a long and hopeless journey. Before looking towards the exact place, he held his breath for a few seconds in order to calm the beating of his heart. The rain began to fall harder, as if it wanted to be present at that special moment. Then Zoltán Wesselényi looked over at

Schubert's tomb and was surprised that it wasn't sepia as in the photographs.

For the first time in his life he'd cried in response to beauty: though he was sensitive, it would never have occurred to him that such a thing was possible. But to hear Margherita singing *Gute Nacht* in that pure, clear voice moved him profoundly. He didn't know that with the very first lines she was announcing what would happen:

Strange, here he came,
Strange, from here I go.

But even when he heard it, no alarm went off. Maybe because he'd always heard it sung by a baritone and Margherita had a crystalline soprano. Or maybe because he was happy, they were happy, sitting in the sun, he on the bench and she on the ground, her head against Zoltán's knee and singing, so that he could hear:

Thou hast not hear my steps,
And I close softly.
I write for thee above the door
To the house "Good night."
Thou shalt know, when taken,
That I think of thee with delight.

They were silent for a long time. He started to cry silently, calmly. A cemetery guard walked discreetly, respectfully, behind them, looked at them perhaps enviously and walked on. Back then there were no groups of tourists in sweatsuits, shouting, chewing gum and trampling on the chrysanthemums.

"You have the most beautiful voice in the world, in life."

She said nothing and looked far away, with her gray eyes, as if she wanted to see to infinity. He insisted:

"Were you listening?"

"Yes."

"Everyone will want to hear you and I'll have to make them stand in line on the street."

She stretched out and looked at him, perhaps with pity. Then Zoltán realized that something was a little bit off .

"What's wrong, Margit?"

And Margherita, *Gute Nacht* still echoing in her ears, explained that she had to leave Vienna at three that afternoon, which is when her train left, and she didn't want him to go to the station to say goodbye because she wouldn't be able to stand it. And she also said, Sorry, sorry, sorry, sorry, sorry, sorry, sorry, like a machine gun. And still she added, Let's say goodbye here, Zoltán. He was open-mouthed with astonishment. Anything was possible but that. He'd been living inside a dream bubble for twenty-eight days, and he'd been such an idiot that he'd never even thought that bubbles of hope always end up bursting in multiple deceptions. Twenty-eight days counted one by one, since they met at a Sunday afternoon concert, behind city hall. She'd just arrived from Vienna, alone, with her far-seeing gray eyes and her sweet laugh. He'd been there for a term, he missed Pest and he fell in love with the voice that asked him, Is this seat taken? He didn't remember what they played, but he found out that Margherita was Venetian; no, she wasn't moldy from the Venetian humidity; she was trying to see if she could get into a voice class at the Hochschule, but it was hard to do, and if she couldn't, she'd go back home and that would be the end of it; she was twenty-two; she didn't like cod, not raw, cooked, dried or any other way; she knew *Sota il ponte de Rialto*, of course, but she hated it, sorry, because she was sick of the tourists; she was alone in Vienna; and so... sooo, yes, she liked him too. Zoltán could hardly breathe; he shyly answered the questions put to him by this woman who seemed still to be propelled by the momentum of travel and answered, Yes; me too; twenty-six; piano, conducting and German; equivalent to the tenth level of piano, yes; Budapest was many travel documents, passports and permits away, but only four hours down the Danube, though four hours were enough to make you feel very lonely; "Mintha szivemböl folyt volna tova, / zavaros, blocs és nagy volt a Duna";[1] yes, foreigners always say that Hungarian is a hard language, but in Pest, Fonvod and Eger children and illiterates can speak it. Yes, Duna is Danube in Hungarian. The Danube has more names than any other river in the world, in life; yes, he often said "in life" when something was huge; oh no, really, my German is still pretty basic. No, I don't know Italian, unfortunately. When the concert ended she said Well, it was nice to meet you, but he said no, he wanted more and she answered, It would be better not to, we should go our separate ways. And Zoltán put his foot down and said, No, and she looked into the distance with her gray eyes and said without looking at him, You don't know me at all, and he answered, I've known you my whole life. And they didn't separate. In twenty-eight days they separated only when he left her at the door of the Hochschule and ran as fast as he could to the Konservatorium to be reminded that he'd have to dedicate thirty hours a day just to the piano to reach the level of the best students, which was the only level possible at the Konservatorium. And now Zoltán didn't feel homesick or sad, because he was walking through the Schubert-Ring or the Stadt-Park with happiness at his side and, as they wandered in no particular direction, he wondered how life could be so happy and Margherita, silent, looking away, penetrated the impossible with her gray eyes and, if she thought she was being looked at, smiled sweetly. He had to let the German classes go, because he needed all the energy left over from the piano to breathe and not die of happiness. And on the twenty-eighth day they were supposed to make a visit to the Zentralfriedhof, where Beethoven, Brahms and company are supposed to be buried. On the streetcar that was taking them to the cemetery she spoke very little, she was distracted, looking out the window and pressing his hand. It was the first day she hadn't been talkative, as if she'd grown up all of a sudden. She had seen infinity.

---

1 "As if its course had begun in my heart, / it was muddy, wise and grand, the Danube" (Attila József).

And now he, sitting on the stone bench, open-mouthed after having heard the most beautiful voice in life singing a song of unhappy love, had had his bubble burst. Why, Margit, why? And she explained, calmly, with almost deathly resignation, that she'd gone to Vienna not to study but to think. Because I wasn't sure if I wanted to get married.

"You're supposed to get married? You?"

"In two weeks."

"Married to whom?"

"To my future husband."

"You have... ?" Zoltán's mouth was still hanging open.

"Yes."

"But you love me!"

"Yes. And him too. I have to marry him." She hesitated and said, "I can finally see things clearly." And after a loaded pause, "I'm sorry."

Now it was Zoltán's black gaze that looked towards infinity. She didn't dare to reproach him; she'd let him get his hopes up because she wouldn't have missed those twenty-eight days of limitless dreaming for anything in the world.

"You're making a mistake, Margit."

"No. I know what I'm doing." She turned to him and put her hand on his knee. "And I know I've hurt you. But it's that I..."

Zoltán made her stop by putting his hand flat over her mouth. And they sat for as long as it took for the shadow of the monument to Mozart to move silently from one side to the other. Suddenly the piano and conducting were of no interest whatever and Pest was no longer a place to be longed for. Suddenly Vienna had become the site of longing, because after three in the afternoon Margit would be gone from there, and the timid luminosity of December would become sad and the streets would no longer make sense because they would lose the trace of his beloved's step. When the shadow of the monument was on the other side, Zoltán, in a hoarse voice:

"We won't see one another again."

"No."

"Where will you be living?"

"I don't know. Venice. And you?"

"Vienna will be unbearable.

"Go back to Budapest." She corrected herself right away. "I mean... do whatever you think you should do..."

Zoltán covered his face with his hands and wept miserably. She let the minutes go by, unhurried, looking at the little puff of steam from Zoltán's breath, though it was almost time for her to leave for the train. He raised his head and tried one more time:

"Fine. But you don't know if you're making a mistake by marrying whoever this is."

"No. We never know if we're making a mistake until we're in it."

"So promise me something."

"What?" Margherita, cautiously.

"If things don't work out... , I'll leave you an address and..."

"No." She cut him off. "I don't want to go behind my husband's back."

"I'm your husband!"

"I don't want to go behind anybody's back."

"You've been going behind my back!" Without looking at her, "What did you do, all those days at the Hochschule?"

"I went in one door and out the other." She said it straight out, but with a kind of gentle humility.

"And then?"

"I'd walk. Think. Until you came."

Zoltán looked away, incredulous, and he didn't say, You shouldn't have lied to me, and she didn't respond, which was a way of accepting that he was right. The sun, saddened by the news, disappeared silently behind a thick layer of white clouds, and the shadow of the monument was extinguished. They didn't notice.

"So promise me something else."

She looked at him, curious, and waited for him to continue.

"Promise me that... twenty-five years from now," he looked at his watch, "on the thirteenth of December at twelve noon ... we'll meet in front of Schubert's tomb."

"Why?"

"After twenty-five years everything's over. But, if we're alive, we can say if we've made a mistake."

She thought it over for a while and then sighed.

"See one another so we can say if we've made a mistake," She smiled from far away. "Fine," she decided.

"Do you promise?"

"I promise."

"Swear it."

"I swear."

Neither of them had the energy to say anything else. The trip back to Vienna on the 72 was even more silent than the trip out. The first snow was threatening to fall from the recently clouded sky. Strangely, it hadn't yet snowed, and the Viennese were casting suspicious glances at the sky as they walked. Margherita got off the streetcar silently, without turning her head, and although they'd gotten to the end of the line, Zoltán kept on looking from the streetcar as she went away, barefoot in the snow, working the hurdy-gurdy, the alms plate quite empty, alone and sad as well.

The rain was streaming down on Vienna's Zentralfriedhof and splattering on Zoltán's umbrella. He stood motionless, looking ahead of him; there was no one in front of Schubert's tomb. Do you really think anybody would be silly enough to honor a pledge made twenty-five years ago? Maybe she's dead. Maybe she lives in Canada. Zoltán didn't want to admit that what bothered him the most was that she might not have come because she hadn't remembered. He knew that forgetfulness was the most painful death.

Zoltán went up to the tomb. A bunch of red roses, destroyed by snows and bad weather, an anonymous tribute, made a note of color against the darkened stone. Layers of old snow were being melted by the rain that tempered the early winter chill, which would turn to cold eventually, though not as slowly, the meteorologists recalled, as a quarter of a century ago when it had been so unseasonably warm.

Anna had died five years ago and he hadn't visited her grave even once. Poor Anna, who never knew that though he loved her tenderly, Zoltán's obsessive gaze passed right over her and focused on the precious memory of Margit, the woman I've been unable to get out of my head because she was framed in just twenty-eight days of breathless love.

Zoltán Wesselényi had been incapable of leaving Vienna after Margit had disappeared. He rented an apartment in the Donaustadt, on the banks of the Danube, to be able to weep and watch the water flow in the Donau, which would become the Duna. He played a couple of memorable recitals at the Konservatorium and became close friends with a couple of fellow students, especially the youngest student in his year, a phenomenon, a music machine who never made a mistake, always tense, his eyes bright, his body almost vibrating. He would say to him, Hey, Peter, music is supposed to make us happy. If happiness grabs you, give up music. And Peter stared at him without understanding or taking his advice, and he called Zoltán a coward, as did the other students, when he decided to stop studying piano on the very day when Herr Reubke was about to tell him that, if he kept on improving at this rate, he would accept him as a student for the following year. But his hands were clenched with sorrow and his soul was dry, and the effort of the classes left him exhausted. So as not to be overwhelmed by unhappiness, he didn't give up conducting, though he knew he'd lost the spark that helps to make the gestures more beautiful and precise, and that allowed him to understand a score at a glance. He went to his classes but he no longer enjoyed them, except for musicology, which allowed him to go through old papers, from centuries before Margit, which was a way of running away without having to go back to Pest empty-handed and hopeless. To make a living he hired himself out as a rehearsal pianist in a little opera theater in Stockerau, met Anna in the office there, married her, and didn't stop thinking about Margit for a single moment in his life.

"You're always sad."

"It's from watching the Duna go by. It makes me melancholy."

"Let's go to Budapest. Your mother would be delighted."

"No. We went there for Christmas. I don't want to spoil her."

"Then let's move."

"No. I want to see the Duna from the balcony."

"What are you thinking about?"

Poor Anna. All the times she asked, not once was he brave enough to tell her that he was thinking about a woman who was both real and a fantasy. He preferred to keep quiet and hold in his sorrow for as long as he could. And Anna was troubled by her husband's dejection, which had no natural explanation. After a few years, Zoltán was supplementing the rehearsal playing by doing research for Professor Bauer of the Vienna Musikwissenschaftzentrum, and earning a pittance which he didn't know how to spend.

He was the delicate one, but it was Anna who died unexpectedly. She was the one who was energetic, never got sick, went to great lengths to avoid conflict. And one day her head hurt, Zoltán, it hurts so much I can hardly see, and in the hospital everyone was very reassuring without ever looking them in the eye and, without more ado, they admitted her. She never left, poor Anna, I cried for her only when she died. A quick death, as if she didn't want to bother those who would stay behind in sorrow, a discreet exit from a woman who had loved him and respected his mysterious unhappiness without insisting on complicated or perhaps impossible explanations.

And after she died, Zoltán never went back to her grave. He went on looking at the Danube from his balcony, his pipe in his hands and his memory of Margit tinged with a profound feeling of guilt because in fifteen years of marriage he'd never laughed or made the slightest effort to laugh, and maybe the lack of laughter at home had helped to form the clot in Anna's brain. Anna, who for so many years had acted as if life were good, everything's fine, one day Zoltán will get over whatever it is and everything will be different, we'll walk along the Prater, we'll go to Heiligenstadt to look at the pretty houses and pretend they're ours, and we'll have chocolate ice cream in Graben, like everybody else.

After Anna's death, which happened at about the same time as Professor Bauer's retirement, Zoltán Wesselényi threw himself desperately into research in order to forget Margit completely, and especially to forget that irritating far-off appointment, which kept his wounds from healing. Also, he was sick of sight reading for second-rate singers worried about their sore throats, who neither looked at him nor thanked him, because the rehearsal pianist is just part of the piano, who always has to be ready, with no sorrows or secret hopes of his own, no need to go and take a piss. He was sick of repeating the same piece ten thousand times, sick of the dirty green of the walls of the rehearsal room where he toiled six hours every day except for Saturdays and Sundays when there was a performance. He was sick of thinking that music was an activity as sad as he was, and he left the little theater without looking back, as Margit had done with him. After devoting a few years to research, he managed to wrap the memory in anesthetic gauze, and he had the two lucky breaks that gave him the prestige he now enjoyed in the field of musicology. He made two finds without setting a foot outside the Musikwissenschaftzentrum of the city of Vienna. One torrentially rainy day, going through a pile of official newspapers from the beginning of the century, he found the slightly mildewed but perfectly legible score of an unknown *Lied* by Schubert, in his own hand, which bore the title *Der Mauersegler* and was dated 1820. With the score was a note from one Mattias Holbein, a tavern keeper from Grinzing, which certified that he had received the score as payment for a night that the seraphic Schubert had spent carousing in his establishment in the company of an impulsive and unidentified young lady. And that the composition was written in his presence in less than an hour, the day after the revels, when the musician found himself short of funds. The ineffectual city employees had misfiled the paper, surely with the intention of cementing the prestige of an unhappy Hungarian musicologist a century and a half later on a torrentially rainy afternoon. The other, much more recent, find, was more significant, because it resulted in changes to many preconceived notions about musical historiography. Among the papers that the organist Kaspar Fischer had bequeathed to the city of Vienna when he died there, at a great age, in 1828, was a score in his hand of a diabolical *Contrapunctum* on the unheard-of theme B-flat, A, D-flat, B, C. The development of the seven variations of this theme was canonical, complete, intelligent, full of ideas, lyrically forceful, confident in the manner of the great masters, and it spoke to the listener in a pan-tonal language eighty years before Schönberg began to think of such things. That masterpiece placed Kaspar Fischer, the author of no other known composition, born in Leipzig but for forty years the humble organist of the Franziskaner-Kirche in Vienna, among the enlightened, among the prophets and geniuses that every art must have from time to time, and it rescued him from an oblivion that would have been terribly undeserved. And it gave Zoltán Wessellyéni a bit of professional prestige, which in fact he did not seek. Too bad Anna hadn't lived to see it. Another stroke of luck broke in on his prayers the day he was playing with Fischer's theme, B-flat, A, D-flat, B, C, the BADESHC theme that had no meaning: he'd been making anagrammatic combinations of the notes when he came on the order D-flat, B-flat, A, C, B. He couldn't relate the letters to one another because the ringing of the telephone distracted him from his obsession. A lucky call: Herr Kreutz informing him that he'd come across a copy of the unobtainable first edition of Laforgue's *Voyage d'hiver*. Naturally, he bought it without haggling over the price, and as he was paging through it, curious to see if it made any reference, however oblique, to the unpublished *Lied*, he came across a kind of bookmark made of very worn leather of an indefinable yellowish color, embossed with a zoological figure. Who knows how long it had been there. The bookmark was placed exactly at the page containing a sepia-colored photo of Schubert's tomb. Immediately the anesthetic gauze dissolved, and all the memories came tumbling down on him. In the photo was a group of people: Gaston Laforgue in the middle, straight as an arrow, covering half the tomb, looking intently at the lens, as if doing so were the most important job in the world; the editor, Schaaf, holding onto his arm; two other men, to whom no reference was made; and a woman, looking away like an absent lover. He stared at the tomb, and Margit's face filled the eyes of his imagination. Not for six more years, Margit, wherever you are. For a few moments he thought that the dreaming woman wasn't part of Laforgue's group: it was Margit, looking for him in the place where they were to meet, sixty years before they knew one another.

The months melted into one another slowly, insipidly, rather meaninglessly, and the prestigious musicologist received the praise, awards, honors and admiration of his colleagues with intimate indifference. Whenever he could, he avoided trips, ceremonies and speeches. He preferred to sit by the window that told him if it was raining or snowing, if the leaves were falling or if it was sunny, to rescue what others had forgotten, he who was incapable of forgetting, as he waited impatiently for time to pass. Peter visited him more than once in the midst of files and scores, and they would talk about music and discoveries, and Zoltán would ask him what it was like always having to be perfect on stage, and Pere Bros, who didn't want to get into it, would answer vaguely, Well, you know, and neither of them would ask for details because modesty prevented one of them from explaining why he was always nervous and the other why he was so sad. But because Zoltán was older, one day he made up his mind and asked, Peter, are you happy, and when he answered, Yes, sure, Zoltán understood it was a lie. That's why he came out with, If someday music doesn't make you happy... we can talk. If you want. And as he said it he was thinking of Margit's harmonious voice.

Zoltán took off his glove and laid his hand flat on the wet seat of the stone bench. As if he expected to feel still the warmth of Margit from twenty-five years ago. Beethoven had no flowers on his tomb. There was a solitary pot with a proud cyclamen at the foot of Brahms's. Who took care of bringing flowers to other people's graves? And was somebody, nowadays, bringing flowers to Anna's? He moved closer to Schubert's grave with the intention of reading the inscription on the stone. Then he realized he couldn't because his eyes were filmed with tears. Until then he hadn't realized that he'd begun to cry when he saw she wasn't there. "In the snow I search in vain for the footprint left behind, when arm-in-arm the two of us would cross the meadow's green," he thought. Had he known it, he would have sung to himself

Is there not even a token
That I can take from here?
When will the sorrow be muted,
Who will bring tidings to me?

In his own baritone voice, as written, but without the life that Margit gave to it.

The *Lied* ended, and he realized that he couldn't hear rain on his umbrella. Water was dripping from the wet trees, but not from the clouds. He held the umbrella aside: only in his eyes was there rain. He closed the umbrella. He still wasn't able to read the inscription on the stone. He wiped his eyes with his handkerchief, and as he bent down, he felt another twinge of backache. That's when he became aware of the swishing. But he was putting on his glasses in order to be able to read the inscription at the foot of the tomb without straining. The swishing grew louder. Zoltán turned around, his glasses down on his nose, a little irritated with whoever was interrupting such an intimate moment. A gray-haired woman wearing an awful yellow raincoat and operating a motorized wheelchair stopped behind him, as if waiting her turn. She had a bunch of white carnations in her lap. Zoltán turned back to the inscription. He lowered his head, raised his chin and read SEINEM ANDENKEN DER WIENER MÄNNERGESANGVEREIN and his mouth fell open. He straightened up and turned around, his mouth still open.

"Zoltán," said the woman in the yellow raincoat.

The gray hair, the deep, gray gaze, the clear skin. Margit, love, my love, I thought you wouldn't come, how fast these twenty-five years have gone by because we're together again as if nothing else has happened.

Zoltán, his mouth still open, removed his glasses.

"Margit." He went up to her and had to lean down to her. "Margit," he repeated, to assure himself of the miracle.

They didn't put carnations on any tombs. She piloted the chair to the stone bench and he followed her, breathing hard. Zoltán sat on the wet surface and they were silent for a long time, as if they both had to recharge the batteries of their memories.

"I made a mistake," she said after a long silence.

"That's what I thought."

They didn't look at one another for fear of the fine, sharp pain of sight.

"And what have you been doing all this time?"

"Going to bed early." Zoltán slowly put his glasses in their case and the case in his overcoat.

"Have you been happy?"

"No. But that wasn't an option. I got married. My wife is dead and I'm very sorry for not having figured out how to be happy with her."

Margherita handed him a white carnation, as if that gesture could console him in his sorrow.

"Poor woman," she sighed.

And they were silent. The monument to Mozart offered no shadow to show the passage of time.

"And you?"

"We separated after two years."

Now he looked at her, upset, surprised.

"Why didn't you come and look for me?"

"I did. But I didn't know where to look. I went to Budapest, downriver, like you said." Margherita's eyes were wide open, but she was looking at her own story, not at the tombs. "How could I find you if I didn't even know your last name? At the Liszt in Pest everybody's called Zoltán."

"I can't believe it." Zoltán's voice was quietly desperate.

"I couldn't find a trace of you. Not a trace. And I ended up living here to be near... the memory of you. Where do you live?"

"You've been living here?" he cried, hurt.

Now Zoltán looked right at her. Her gray eyes hurt him and showed how painfully sharp a look can be.

"For the last twenty years. I stopped singing and stopped having anything to do with music because…"

He interrupted her. "You've been living in Vienna for twenty years?"

"In Heiligenstadt. Thinking of you."

Zoltán stood up and exhaled, incredulous. He sat down again.

"In Heiligenstadt," he said, to confirm it.

"Yes."

"In a pretty house." He shook his head, perplexed. "Anna used to say…" He shook his head again to mean he had nothing more to say, he gave up, she should talk.

"Yes, it's a pretty house. Near Beethoven's. But after the accident I moved downtown, to a building with an elevator."

Now Zoltán focused for the first time on the wheelchair. He opened his mouth to say something, but his same thought obsessed him.

"Twenty years sharing traffic lights and the ferris wheel at the Prater."

"I've never gone up there. I didn't know you were here."

"Twenty years. Did you get married again?"

No. But I've found…" She stopped and changed the topic. "I looked for you until…"

"Why did you leave me," Zoltán interrupted her, deeply wounded, "if you were going to miss me so much?"

"I've always been like that. But I never knew why."

"And now?"

"Now I know."

"Why?"

She picked up the bunch of carnations, looked at it and put it back on her lap, uncomfortable.

"How's the piano?"

"I quit. I became a rehearsal pianist."

"You were very good."

"Yes, but I didn't have…" He stopped. "You haven't explained why you left me if you were going to miss me so much."

She said nothing. As if it were hard for her to be honest with Zoltán. After a long pause:

"It's that... it scares me to hold onto happiness. It burns, I'm afraid it'll explode."

He put his hand between hers, to hold onto.

"Here. It won't explode."

But instinctively she opened her hands and let him go.

"I've come here many times," she said, to hide her agitation. "But it's been a while... I've found..."

"I never have. Ever, until today." He looked around, as if asking the wet surroundings to be a witness. "I couldn't have stood it."

Margit said nothing and decided to change the subject.

"Do you have children?"

"No. I have memories. Can I ask you to lunch?"

"It's... This is a little... I have problems..." She pointed to the wheelchair as if it were to blame. "... with bladder control. I don't like to be away from home for too long."

"We'll do whatever you say."

She thought for a few seconds. It seemed to Zoltán that the woman's gray eyes were regaining the penetrating power of her encounters with the mysteries.

"Let me go to the bathroom. Then..." She smiled. "Then we'll see."

Zoltán stood up and she went to his side. A few drops started to fall. They went towards the building at the entrance, where the restrooms were, in silence. Outside the bathroom, she turned the chair towards him and looked into his eyes.

"Wait for me here."

"I've always done what you say." He looked at her seriously. "Why shouldn't I do it now?"

She winked a gray eye and disappeared through the door to the handicapped section. Zoltán turned around and sighed. He wasn't satisfied; he was shaken. He smelled the white carnation Margherita had given him. He breathed in the scent hard, optimistically. If he'd been able to achieve some kind of serenity over the years, now the whole thing was falling down around his ears. The drops were coming faster now. He put the carnation in his buttonhole with impulsive coquetry and, his hands free, opened the umbrella and once again heard the patter on the fabric. But now it sounded sweet to him because there was hope in it.

After a few minutes the rain stopped as it had started and he closed the umbrella again. Then the vibration of the phone told him that the world was still turning. Peter's distant voice woke him from his dream.

"Hey, Peter," he said indifferently, "what do you want?"

"No, nothing, just thanks for the book about Fischer. I've only been able to flip through it, but you can tell it's amazing."

"Come on." Inexcusably impatient. "What's wrong?"

"I can't play. And I can't not play. I think about you a lot. I'm sad, Zoltán."

"Listen, right now I'm..."

"I haven't slept in six months because I'm so upset. I need some rest. And you told me..."

"Listen, why don't we talk some other time?"

"If music keeps you from being happy, quit music, you told me."

"Listen, we'll talk about this, all right?"

"I've seen Schubert." Peter's desperate voice.

"Schubert?" Instinctively, Zoltán looked towards the tomb. But he went back immediately to watching the door to the handicapped stalls.

"Peter, listen. I..."

"Fine, fine."

"Call me some other time, all right?"

"I love you. With all my heart. Remember that."

Peter hung up, too brusquely perhaps, and Zoltán had to do the same, thoughtfully. What had he wanted to say? Just as he was about to conclude that Pere Bros had big problems, he was distracted by a chubby individual coming out of the men's restroom, whom he hadn't seen go in. He concentrated on his door and forgot about his friend's distant lament because the throbbing of his recovered hope blocked it out. He couldn't act like a big brother when his heart was exploding. He started walking back and forth in front of the restrooms, patient and impatient, thinking about important things like, for example, it was inexcusable that in their time together he still hadn't asked her what had happened, why she was in a wheelchair. What's that about an accident, Margit, what happened to you?

He was distracted by a couple his age with a young, pretty girl, maybe their daughter. They'd just come through the gate and he deduced from their gestures as they looked at a map that they were looking for the tombs on his side. He felt envious of them. He followed them with his eyes as they went in the right direction. He looked, almost annoyed, at the restroom doors. Of course, if she couldn't manage, poor Margit... It was starting to rain again. He examined the sky and his watch and exhaled with some impatience. Instead of opening the umbrella again, he opened the door to the bathrooms and stepped into a corridor with two closed doors.

"Margit?"

Nobody answered.

"Margherita?"

He pushed hard on one of the doors. The stall was empty.

"Margit?" His voice more rattled.

He pushed the other door. That stall was empty too. Now he shouted.

"Margit!"

Back in the corridor, he realized that there was another door in the back wall. He ran to it. It opened onto the lobby. He asked the guard if he'd seen a lady in a wheelchair, wearing some yellow thing, and the guard, showing a tooth broken by life, said, Yes, a lady with gray hair, very elegant, very beautiful. And Zoltán, grasping his wrist, Exactly! And the guard: Well, she just left in a taxi that was waiting for her. Going where? To Vienna. Is there a taxi stand? Not here. Farther on, where the bus stops, there is. The best thing is the streetcar, if you want to go back to Vienna.

Zoltán hadn't heard the last part because he'd started running desperately in the direction of Vienna, hoping to catch a stray taxi.

He heard the bell of the 72 when he was almost at the stop. He got on and went to the front, to calm his impatience.

He made the trip with his eyes open and his lungs aching. They didn't pass any taxis, the windows of the streetcar were steaming up, and he was coming to terms with a new loss. Two taxis crossed their path and Margit was in neither of them. When they got to the end of the line, next to the Ring, Zoltán, all hope gone, didn't get off the streetcar as he'd done on the day she left him forever for the first time. Despondent, he started to cry and the lively smell of the white carnation in his lapel came to him in a cruel whiff. Margit had sunk out of sight again. Margit, whom he knew only as Margherita, who always ran away from happiness and now lived in a downtown apartment, in a building with an elevator.

The conductor glanced at him in the rearview mirror, but decided not to look for trouble just yet. Zoltán straightened up and, with a deep sigh, leaned back against the seat. Then he leaned his head towards the steamy, dirty window, as if he were a night owl coming back from an especially hard night, his tie askew, the cheery carnation hanging from his buttonhole, his eyes bleary as an alcoholic's. Because the music to Thou hast not to hear my steps, and I close softly. I write for thee above the door to the house "Good night" was playing in his head, he shakily wrote Good night, Margit on the steamy glass, so you know I thought of you. Through the letters, Zoltán glimpsed the old man walking barefoot on the icy ground, his hurdy-gurdy in his hand, recalling distant moments of happiness, and he started to sing, to the indignation of the conductor, who now stood up angrily with the intention of kicking that drunk off his streetcar. Zoltán sang from the deepest sorrow, in his insecure baritone voice, Old man of the stories, shall I walk with thee? When I sing my verses, wilt thou play with me? He let the tears fall from his eyes as he looked unseeing through the letters written on the glass at a piece of the city that would be even more unbearable now, though he knew he would not leave it. As the conductor was telling him to behave and get off the vehicle, from the depths of his forgotten memory came a B-flat, A, D-flat, B, C that he'd carried inside for years, Kaspar Fischer's theme urging him to look forward, be brave, believe himself capable of remaking the future, as if it were the main theme of his Hymn to the Ability to Live without Thinking about Beloved Margit. He rejected the idea as he yielded to the conductor's appeals and got up fromhis seat. He couldn't emulate a prophet like Kaspar Fischer; he was just a person.

Then he understood that there was no choice, that he couldn't leave Vienna, that life is not the road or even the destination, but the journey, and when we disappear it's in the middle of the trip, wherever that may be. It was his bad luck that his lot was a hard winter journey that had left his soul in ruins.

Epilogue

The stories in this collection were written over a relatively long period of time. The oldest, in its first version, dates from 1982, and all were finished in 2000. What's interesting is that I never got them right the first time. With one exception, the original version didn't turn out to be the one I considered definitive. In many cases the themes and issues were right, but the tone was still off. For years I've felt somewhat perplexed about what turned out to be these pages, because I had stories and ideas, but I wasn't pleased with what I made of them. Once, after finishing *The Shadow of the Eunuch*, on which I'd spent many years, I started working hard on the stories, thinking that the time had come to demystify them and make them mine. But I had to recognize, after many fruitless sessions, that either these stories had no reason to exist or I had no reason to exist for them. When I finally understood that stories have legs, I changed tactics, and as Lao Tse recommends—according to Quiquín—I sat quite still outside my cabin door and waited until one day the stories passed by, and I grabbed them by the throat and made them explain themselves. So, with great patience, I figured out the secret of each story, one by one, the reason why the first line or first word of a story had occurred to me or maybe the precise or vague idea of a literarily edifying ending that could exist only in relation to a beginning that I didn't yet know. The final versions, new versions of the majority of the fourteen stories, have brought me many surprises. Maybe the biggest surprise is the realization that everything in life is related. I thought I was putting together a collection of totally independent stories, since the ambience of each story demanded this independence, but the reality of working on them these last few months, in the same span of time, has made me aware of the threads, some secret and others more obvious, that tie them all to one another. I also got to know and, in a way, to love characters who exist without the advantages enjoyed by characters in novels, because living in a story is like spending your whole life in one of those Japanese hotels that seem like a decompression chamber for divers. These characters, like their stories, are often based on what is, but is not said.

There have been low points along the way. There was something about a couple of the stories that just wasn't right and I left them out, though I didn't get rid of them. I imagine them in limbo, waiting for better times.

I think that readers of stories have to be more attentive than readers of novels. The space limitations that I referred to above lead to omissions, force the writer to make assumptions about previous lives, summarize entire moral or physical descriptions in a single stroke... The writer must be ingenious, but so must the reader. The writer suggests background, history, landscape, atmosphere, and the reader completes these suggestions in the act of reading. And because not everything can fit into a story, the resulting echo, the memory of reading (equivalent to the immediate auditory memory of music) ends up completing the moral dimension of each story, if there is one.

I realized these things as I worked on this book, as I've also realized that how you breathe when you write a story is different, more syncopated, than the breathing required to write a novel, because it seems as if you have to win the game going in, convincingly and right off the bat, rather than settling in for the long, speculative, laborious, tactical combat of the novel, which you can win on points. Again I refer to Quiquín when he cites the Baron of Coubertin, who was inspired by Saint Paul (his second letter to Timothy of Listra, his faithful disciple), when he stated that in art what matters is winning, and everything else is just a tale.

I am deeply grateful to Miquel Desclot for the magnificent gift of the unpublished versions of Wilhelm Müller's *Die Winterreise*, which appear quoted and in less obvious ways in the story *Winterreise*.

The Catalan version of the two lines from the great Hungarian poet Attila Jószef which appear in that story are from Eduard J. Verger and Kálmán Faluba. Sr. Adrià, who provided me with the reference, confirms that the book is *Poemes* (Ed. Gregal, Valencia, 1987).

Winterreise is a posthumous cycle of lieder composed by Franz Schubert on a book of poems by Wilhelm Müller entitled *Die winterreise*. Attilio Bertolucci left us a collection of poems called *Viaggio d'inverno*. Some years ago, Antoni Marí wrote a book of poems, twelve songs, that bears the title *Un viatge d'hivern*. The questionable biography of Franz Schubert written by Gaston Laforgue, more to serve himself than to serve the music, is called *Voyage d'hiver*. From the moment that these stories began to assume an imprecise shape, I knew that the collection would have to be called *Winter Journey*. Some coincidences are intentional and others are not, and even if inevitable they can sometimes be unwelcome. I hope that in this case Müller, Schubert, Bertollucci, Laforgue and Marí will take this book as homage.

Also, I want to record a series of dedications that I hope will be received with, at least, resignation: Gottfried Heinrich's Dream" I dedicate to Martí Cabré Barba; a very old first version was already related to him. "With Hope in His Hands" was born dedicated to Clara Cabré Barba. "I Remember" had its origin in a lively conversation with Sam Abrams and is dedicated to him. "Opus Postum" is dedicated to Cristòfol A. Trepat, who knows what it is to go on stage, and to Montserrat Guixer, as well as to the tireless Jordi Mir. "Two Minutes," which bites its own tail, is for Jan Schejbal, of Prague, and Ramón Pla i Arxé, of Barcelona. "Eyes Like Jewels" is for Joaquim M. Puyal, eternally enraptured by the miracle of language, and for Til Stegmann, of Frankfurt, and Joan F. Mira, of Castelló, conspirators in Münster. "Negotiation," which in the end is without music because of the pianist's unilateral retirement, to my musical comrades-in-arms Josep Lluís Badal, Oriol Costa and Jaume Sala. "Ballad" is an old story that remained almost faithful to the original idea and is intended for Josep M. Ferrer and Magda Calpe, and for Jaume Aulet. "Dust," not because of the dust but because of the books, is for Ton Albes and Lluïsa Carbonell. To my siblings I dedicate "The Trace." "Finis Coronat Opus" is for Xavier Fabré and Marta Nadal. "The Will" is for Kálmán Faluba, of Budapest, and for Adolf Pla, of Sabadell, "Poc!" despite its violence, is for Oriol Izquierdo and Dolors Borau and for Sergi Boadella. "Winterreise" is for Margarida Barba.

Jaume Cabré
Fall 2000

Translator's Note

Readers unfamiliar with Jaume Cabré need to know two fundamental facts about him. First, he is a native speaker of Catalan who writes in his own language. And second, he is the author of novels and short stories that have an enthusiastic readership not just in Catalonia but in much of Europe.

Most authors write in their native language; exceptions to this generalization, such as Beckett and Nabokov, are famously few. Why then is the fact that Jaume Cabré writes in his own language worthy of mention? The answer is bound up with the minority status of Catalan, a language spoken by some seven million Spaniards, about one-sixth of the population of Spain. Catalan is protected by the Spanish constitution of 1978, but Spanish has the geopolitical advantage of being both a national and a world language. Because Catalan and Spanish are related languages (both are descended from Latin) and because Spanish was vigorously promoted during the Franco dictatorship (1939–1975), virtually all speakers of Catalan are bilingual.

Bilingualism is a very complex phenomenon, and the unique characteristics of an individual's bilingualism are the result of where the languages are used (at home, in school, in public interactions, on radio and television, etc.) and what they are used for (to converse, to read and write, to do business, to relax, etc.). Some of the writers who have been formed by Catalan/Spanish bilingualism, notably

Juan Marsé and Eduardo Mendoza, write in Spanish. Jaume Cabré writes in Catalan.

The choice of a literary language entails both advantages and disadvantages. On the plus side, Catalan is the natural expression of Cabré's personal and intellectual history. And using Catalan is a conscious act of support for a language whose vitality is far from guaranteed. The disadvantage of writing in Catalan, however, is obvious: an author as creative and as prolific as Cabré (he also writes essays, television and movie scripts and children's literature) would be much better known, and much more marketable, if he wrote in Spanish. He would be writing in a language that has nearly 400 million speakers, and for which there is an established network of editors, translators and publishers. In spite of this disadvantage, Cabré has achieved both critical and popular success, and his work has attracted a wide readership. His 2004 novel about the aftereffects of the Spanish civil war, *Les veus del Pamano* (*Voices of the Pamano*), was the toast of the 2007 Frankfurt Book Fair, at which Catalan culture was the Guest of Honor. He is well known in Europe, and his works have been translated into fourteen languages.

Winter Journey is the first of Jaume Cabré's works to be translated into English. Imaginative and accomplished, it needs no special pleading. But any work written in Catalan is part of the ongoing project of saving the language, and the culture of which it is a central part, from being worn away by assimilation. I hope that my translation will serve this work both as literature and as Catalan literature.

Winter Journey is an atypical collection of short stories. Many collections bring together stories that were written over a given period of time, but these stories were written at different times and—as Cabré explains in the Epilogue—were brought together only when he figured out what they had in common. Nor do these stories share a single style; the collection includes international intrigue (*Poc!*), fantasy (*Dust*), historical narrative (*With Hope in His Hands*), interior monologue (*Finis Coronat Opus*) and even O.

Henry-esque fable (*The Will*). Rather, the stories in *Winter Journey* share motifs, obsessions, objects, and even some characters. One side of a phone conversation appears in the first story, for example, and the other side in the last. An embossed leather bookmark belonging to Bach in *Gottfried Heinrich's Dream* shows up centuries later in the collection of an eccentric bibliophile in *Dust*. And so on... Readers will want to discover other connections themselves.

The stories do not share a time and place; they are set in various European countries and in various centuries, but painting (especially Rembrandt's *The Philosopher*) and music (especially Schubert's *Winterreise*) play a role in almost all of them. Some of the characters are artists or musicians, many of them are seekers of aesthetic pleasure, and a few do terrible things in the pursuit of beauty. Taken together, the stories are a discourse on beauty: its power, its danger, and its price. Given that music has been a theme in many of Cabré's works, the collection might be thought of as a set of variations on the theme of beauty.

This translation presented several challenges. One was the specialized vocabulary; references to music, for example, range from classical repertory to parts of the organ to King Crimson. These references had to be as unobtrusive in the translation as they are in the original work: details that serve to define the characters but that do not otherwise call attention to themselves. Not all of the clues will be picked up on by all readers, but they had to be there to be found by readers who share the interests of the characters. An additional challenge was that each story was a new text, and therefore a new occasion for negotiating the nature of the translation's faithfulness to the original. Finally, the stories had to be as enjoyable in English as they are in Catalan; they are sophisticated and intellectual, but also fun to read, and I tried to retain this quality in the translation. In fact, reading is one of the aesthetic pleasures that fuel the actions of the characters of *Winter Journey*.

I began to learn Catalan as a graduate student in Hispanic linguistics, and had the good fortune to study with the Catalan linguist Josep Roca-Pons and to become friends with him and with his wife, Teresa. Thanks to them, I learned to speak Catalan, but after I became a professor of Spanish my Catalan ebbed and flowed depending on my access to speakers of the language. In 2007 I was in Barcelona, collaborating with colleagues at the Universitat Pompeu Fabra and trying to perfect my Catalan. As part of this effort I started looking for a work of Catalan literature that I might translate, and a chain of contacts led me to *Viatge d'hivern*, which has become *Winter Journey*. I am grateful to Jaume Cabré for authorizing this translation and for answering my questions without betraying the slightest dismay at what I didn't know; to Carme Rei-Granger for introducing me to *Viatge d'hivern*; to Maria Roura-Mir for advice about translation; and to Josep and Teresa Roca-Pons for sharing with me their profound knowledge and love of their language.

Swan Isle Press is an independent, not-for-profit, literary
publisher dedicated to publishing works of poetry, fiction
and nonfiction that inspire and educate while advancing the
knowledge and appreciation of literature, art, and culture.
The Press's bilingual editions and single-language English
translations make contemporary and classic texts more
accessible to a variety of readers.

For information on books of related interest or for
a catalog of new publications contact:

www.swanislepress.com

Winter Journey
Designed by Esmeralda Morales-Guerrero
Typeset in Calluna 11/14
Printed on 55# Glatfelter Natural